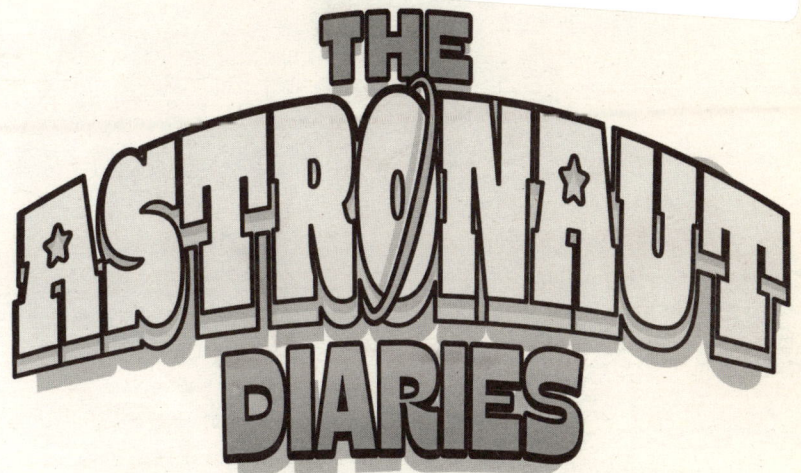

THE ASTRONAUT DIARIES

Journal of Andi Futura, aged 11 1/2

BY ASTRONAUT
Samantha Cristoforetti
and Emma Roberts

CHAPTER ONE

9:00 am (400 km above Earth)

For my seventh birthday, my dad stuck glow-in-the-dark stars on my bedroom ceiling. Dad told me my stars were in the shape of the Andromeda constellation, and that was super cool because I was named after those stars: Andromeda Futura. (But everyone just calls me Andi.)

It was that same day I decided I would become an astronaut so I could see the real stars up close.

Now I'm **SO** much older (11½) and guess what? I'm here! I'm writing my diary from **actual** space! I mean, technically I'm not an astronaut yet, but both my parents are, and my big brother Perri – which is short for Perigee; the point in the moon's orbit around Earth when it's nearest Earth (my parents love a theme) – has just finished his astronaut training.

For this mission, I'm what's known as a **"spaceflight participant"**, which basically means I'm here as a passenger only. I mean, I've done some training back on Earth, like:

 Preparing for weightlessness in a special plane called a "Zero-G aircraft" (AKA "The Vomit Comet", because things can get a bit queasy up there!)

 What to do in a whole bunch of emergencies that probably won't happen (but just in case!)

 Sessions in a simulator so I could feel what launch and re-entry would feel like (more on that later!)

Oh, and also how to do basic stuff like use space toilets, because even spaceflight participants need to be able to do that! It sounds a lot, but my months of training were nothing like the hard work actual astronauts have put in, as they've often trained for years before going on a mission.

But here's the really cool bit: Ms Asimov, my tutor at Mission Control Centre back on Earth, has promised that **IF** I do eight assignments and find a mission to complete while I'm on the International Space Station, she'll let me start astronaut training properly when we get back home.

I'D BE THE YOUNGEST ASTRONAUT-IN-TRAINING EVER!

Anyway, hello, dearest diary. And you already know just how dear you are, as I chose to pack you in my **Personal Preference Kit (PPK)** before we left for the ISS. That's what we call the small box everyone in the crew is given to stash the special things they want to bring into space. It's no bigger than the lunch box I used to take to school, but I've managed to cram in some great stuff. I've got...

Extra socks

Because we aren't walking around on the ground like we are on Earth, we don't need to wear shoes on the ISS. Instead we wear socks to keep our feet warm.

My favourite book

I've read it 42 times!

DOUGLAS ADAMS
The Hitchhiker's Guide to the Galaxy

A piece of stromatolite

Mum gave me this. Cool fact: 3.7 billion years ago, when Earth was just a baby planet, these rock-like mounds were being made all over the place by the earliest bacterial life forms. Now I can look at Earth while holding a really old piece of it!

My favourite T-shirt

It's signed by my best friends. They're super excited that their names have made it into space!

Kelsi
Dorian
Ava
Audrey

Things I Wasn't Allowed to Bring

🫤 **Cookies** – if any crumbs floated off and got into the electrics that would be BAD... Although in 1965 an astronaut managed to smuggle a corned beef sandwich on board the Gemini 3 spacecraft!

😵 **Nail polish** – flammable. Also bad.

🫤 **Smartphone** – waaaah.

Perri refuses to tell me what's in his PPK, but I know Dad packed our family camera in his; Douglas, our dog, has his favourite toy; and Mum brought a photo of Nan on her allotment as well as a stash of the boiled sweets she always gets from the shop at the end of our street. Mum said the point of a PPK is to bring things that remind us of what we love and who we are back home. You can sometimes feel a bit... *disconnected* from everything up here, and our PPK stuff helps us to feel happier.

Okay, I've got to do a space-to-ground video chat with Ms Asimov and find out what my first assignment is. Back soon.

1:00 pm

My first assignment is SO awesome. ☺ Ms Asimov
wants me to draw a plan of the ISS and label the places I think are the most interesting. I get to draw *and* explore! The only trouble is, I haven't quite got to grips with this whole floating-in-microgravity* thing yet, and I keep bashing into stuff. At least there're plenty of handholds on the walls to grab on to and push off from. (And Perri and I love hanging upside down like bats from the ones in the ceiling when we eat!)

Mum told me I need to be super delicate as I push myself along the walls of the ISS, like I'm pushing on a bubble but trying not to pop it.

I'm more out-of-control elephant than delicate at the moment, but I'm working on it, Mum.

* Okay, this might sound weird, but microgravity is when you feel like you're floating when actually, you're FALLING! Here's how it works: on Earth, gravity is the force that pulls everything down. It's what keeps your feet on the pavement when you're out for a walk, and it's why that plate of toast you knocked off the kitchen counter when you were rushing to leave for school will always land on the floor. The falling-not-floating thing is because the ISS – and all of us inside it – moves really fast as it orbits Earth at a speed that means we can match Earth's curve (28,165 kph to be precise!). So, while Earth's gravity is always trying to pull us down and therefore we're constantly falling, we're falling *around* the planet, not down to it.

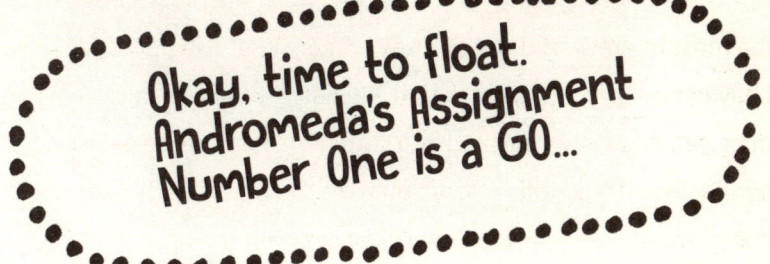

Okay, time to float.
Andromeda's Assignment
Number One is a GO...

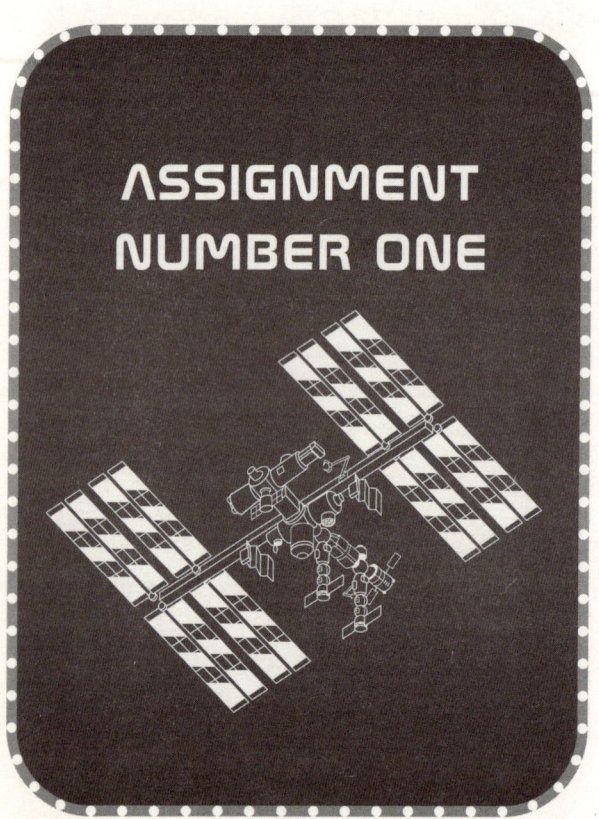

ASSIGNMENT
NUMBER ONE

All Aboard the International Space Station

· ·

The ISS is our home *and* office (for Mum and Dad) for the next few months. It's made up of sections called **"modules"** that were brought up here and put together in space ages before I was even born. Different modules are run by the space agencies from different countries: the ESA in Europe; NASA in America; CSA in Canada; JAXA in Japan, and Roscosmos in Russia. But everyone gets along just great on board!

Modules

With all the modules put together, the volume inside for us crew is about the same as a jumbo jet. The modules have awesome names too, like **Destiny, Harmony, Tranquility,** and **Columbus**.

(1) **Destiny**   (3) **Tranquility**

(2) **Harmony**   (4) **Columbus**

Kibo

The largest module on the Space Station, *Kibo*, means "Hope". 💚 It's run by the Japan Aerospace Exploration Agency (JAXA).

(4)

Dragon

This spacecraft launches from the USA. Some Dragons just bring supplies, but some can transport up to seven crew. It's how we got here!

Solar panels

Enormous solar panels rotate to absorb as much sunlight as possible. This can then be converted into electricity to power the ISS.

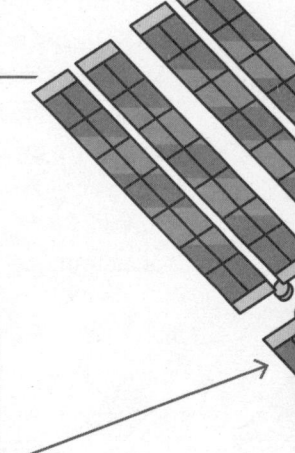

Robotic Arm

These looooong robot arms can grab the cargo vehicles sent from Earth every few months (they're the ones that bring fresh food and everything else we need up to the ISS – it's like a space delivery service 😊). They can also move equipment and supplies around and help astronauts with their work outside the ISS.

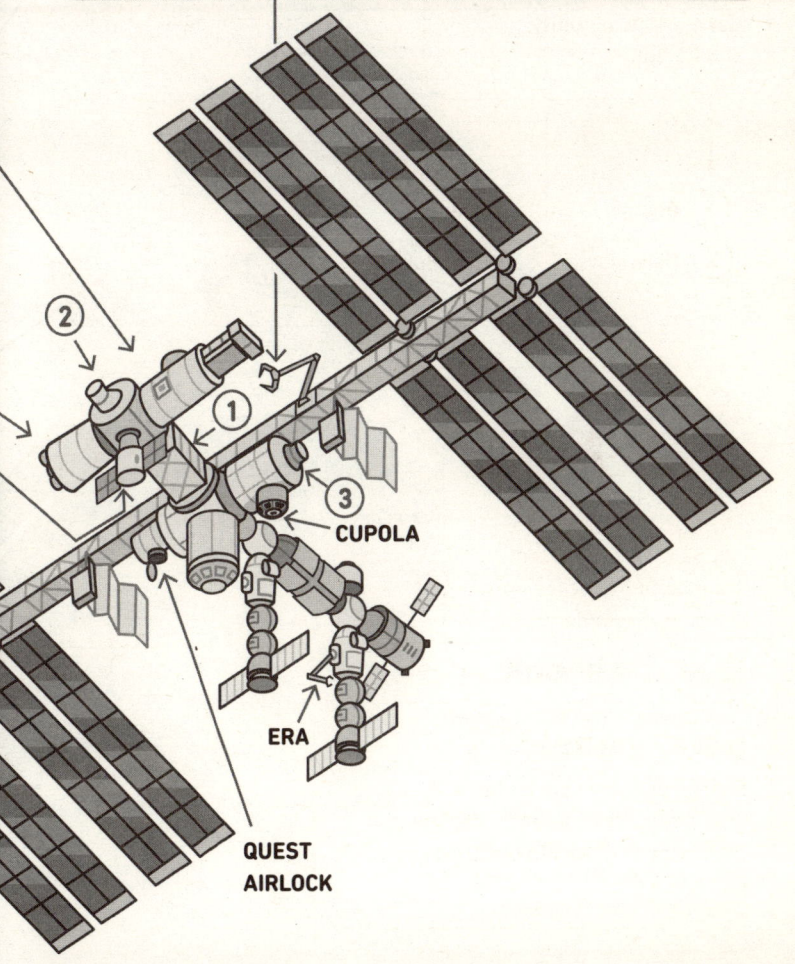

② ①

③ CUPOLA

ERA

QUEST
AIRLOCK

Columbus Lab

The ISS is basically one massive laboratory with experiments going on all the time. But there are also dedicated labs, like this one, run by the European Space Agency (ESA).

Quest Airlock

This is where astronauts go out on EVAs – the fancy name for spacewalks. There are two units inside: one for getting into your spacesuit and prepping your tools, and the other with the actual hatch out to space.

Tranquility

This is a module containing lots of useful things, like a toilet and a treadmill. I definitely won't be using one while someone else is using the other. 😊

TOILET

TREADMILL

Cupola

My favourite place on the ISS – it's like a viewing gallery for Earth and the stars. I'd spend all day in there if I could, just gazing out of the windows.

4:00 pm

I'm back! And I didn't bash into too much stuff on my way... I even managed to stop for a milk candy in Kibo with the Japanese crew (and Douglas got a sardine, which means Kibo is now his new favourite place).

My drawing is all done and ready to deliver to Mission Control Centre. Two drawings, to be precise, as I think the inside is just as interesting as the outside on the ISS. Maybe Ms Asimov will give me extra credit? And maybe she'll be so impressed she'll let me go on a spacewalk before we go home...

Oh! That's it, dear diary! My mission! The one I have to complete to qualify early for Astronaut-in-Training.

Drum roll, please...

Before we leave the ISS to return to Earth in six months time, I, Andromeda Futura, aged 11½, will have been on an EVA. Now I just need to find a way to convince everyone else that this is a mostly harmless idea...

Writing in Space

Oh, and just a little extra fact before I put you away for today, diary: In 1966, a space pen was invented that could write in weightlessness. It uses pressurised nitrogen to force the ink out into the nib.

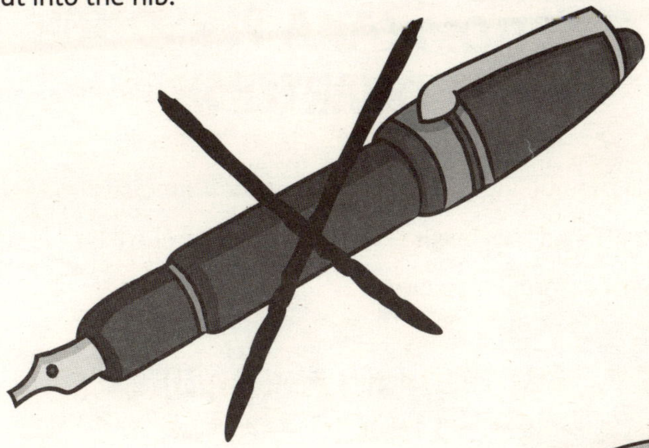

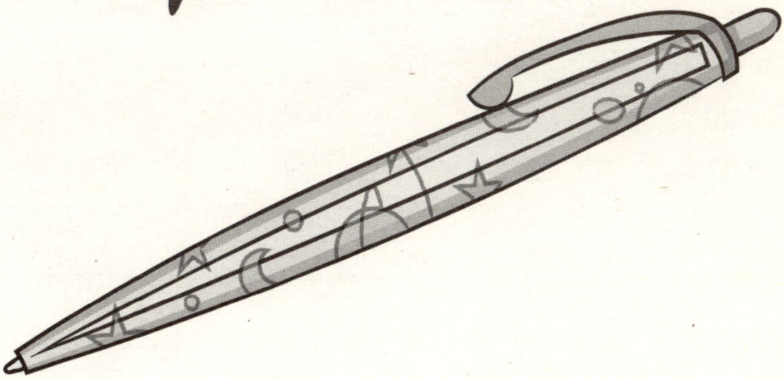

But I'm just using a regular old pencil. Sometimes the littlest things remind you of home. ☺

CHAPTER TWO

MY BEDROOM (AKA PERSONAL CREW QUARTERS)

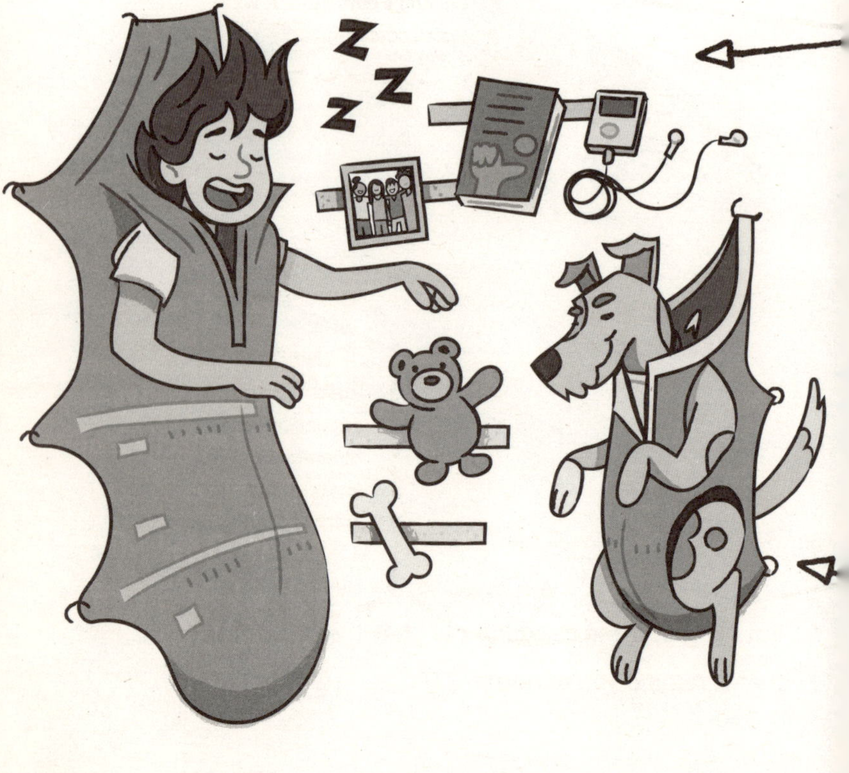

Microgravity = no sinking into soft mattresses or squidgy pillows. Instead, we strap ourselves to the wall so we don't bump about while we're catching Zs.

A sleeping bag with holes means our arms can flooooaaaat gently in front of us. It's actually pretty relaxing!

7:30 am

We've been here a few weeks now and I'm just about getting used to this whole microgravity thing. Still not used to having to wear my sleeping bag, though! ☺)

So, diary, I've been awake for *hours* already, and it has been totally worth it... This morning, a resupply spacecraft arrived from Earth, **AND** I got to watch Dad catch it with the robotic arm! We'll be unpacking the goodies from the craft later, but it'll be full of all sorts of equipment for the amazing experiments that are always happening up here, plus loads of supplies for the crew as well. **I'm hoping someone squeezed in some extra milk candy!**

Dad said there'll be new spacecraft arriving a couple of times a year to the International Space Station. Some, like the Cygnus spacecraft, don't have people on board – they just bring cargo, dock for a bit, and then get packed with all the rubbish from the International Space Station before leaving to burn up in Earth's atmosphere. Others, like a Soyuz, bring crew **AND** a bit of cargo, but there's not much room in there for carrying lots of things back to Earth.

And then there are the two types of Dragon spacecraft – one for carrying cargo and one for crew. Dragons don't get burned up. They can carry **tonnes** of astronauts' stuff and results from experiments on the ISS safely back to Earth and then get used again.

Watching Dad catch the spacecraft this morning got me thinking about the Crew Dragon that brought us here. It was a totally **epic** journey. In fact, the whole of Launch Day was **epic**. Here's how it went:

Launch-minus 5 hours: We had a special family meal of Italian focaccia bread and cheese omelettes. We'd been in quarantine together for two weeks by then to stop us taking any germs or sickness into space. Every day, our amazing chefs cooked us whatever we wanted to eat. Mum still made me and Perri have our veggies though.

L-minus 4 hours: We got into our spacesuits, which were designed by an actual Hollywood movie costume designer! They are custom made for each of us, so they fit perfectly. Perri complained about having to wear a MAG – Maximum Absorbency Garment (basically a nappy) – underneath, but I reminded him of Dad's favourite story about the first American astronaut to go to space. He wasn't given a MAG, and he had such a long wait for launch that he had to pee in his suit and short-circuited all the medical sensors inside! Perri stopped complaining after that.

23

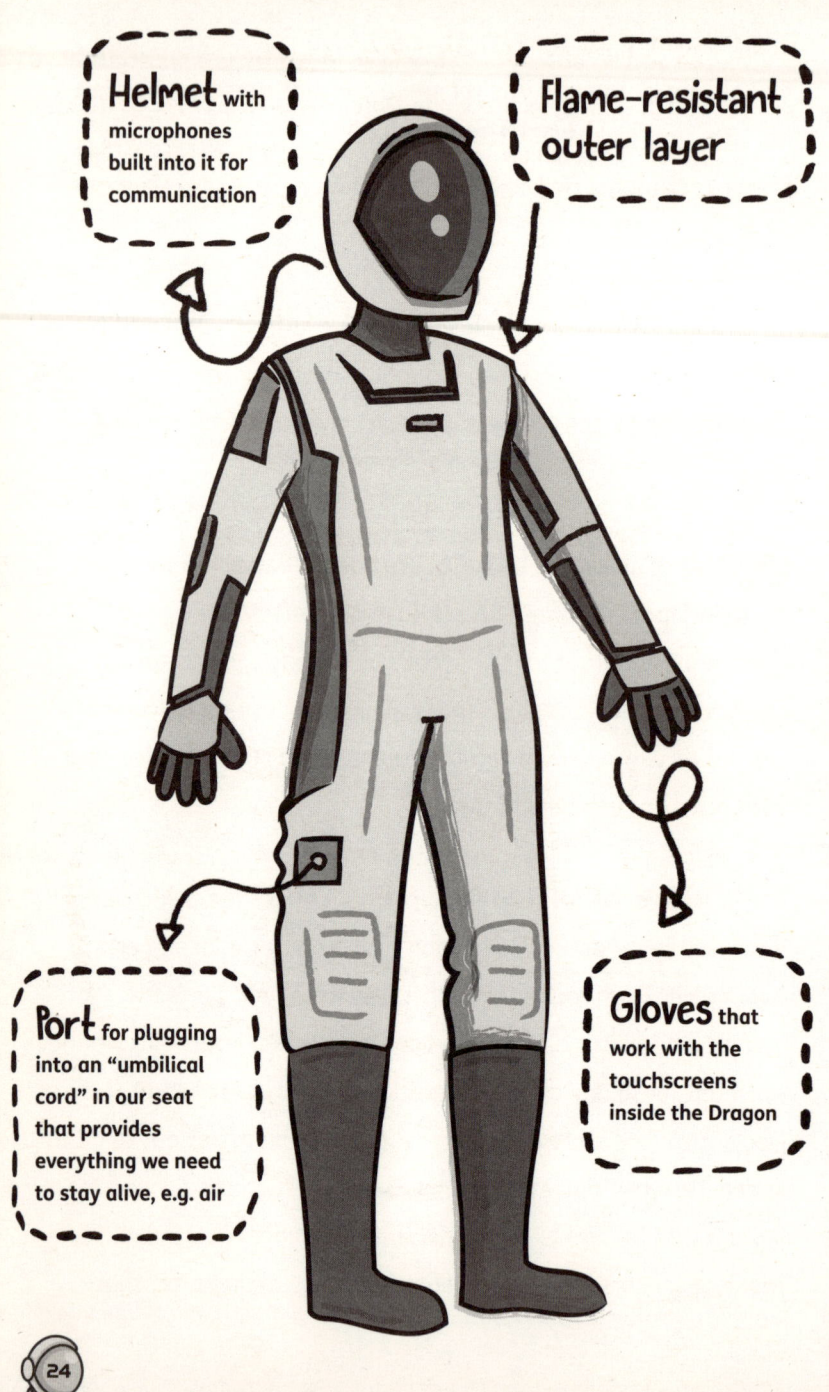

L-minus 3 hours 10 minutes: We were driven to the launch pad in a fancy electric car. Dad insisted we listen to a playlist he'd made, which – even though Dad's musical taste is **SO old-fashioned** – was actually pretty perfect. ☺

Rocket Man — Elton John

Across the Universe — The Beatles

Walking on the Moon — The Police

Space Oddity — David Bowie

I always thought this song was by the astronaut who took his guitar to space and recorded himself singing it. I've watched it on YouTube like 1,000 times! Mum said that crew sometimes leave instruments on the space station for other astronauts to use when they've gone. I really hope the guitar's still there.

L-minus 2 hours 50 minutes: We popped Douglas into his crate and got in the lift all the way up to the crew access arm. It's basically a tunnel suspended about 65 metres off the ground that leads to the Dragon capsule, which is now sitting in place on top of the Falcon 9 rocket that will help us blast into space.

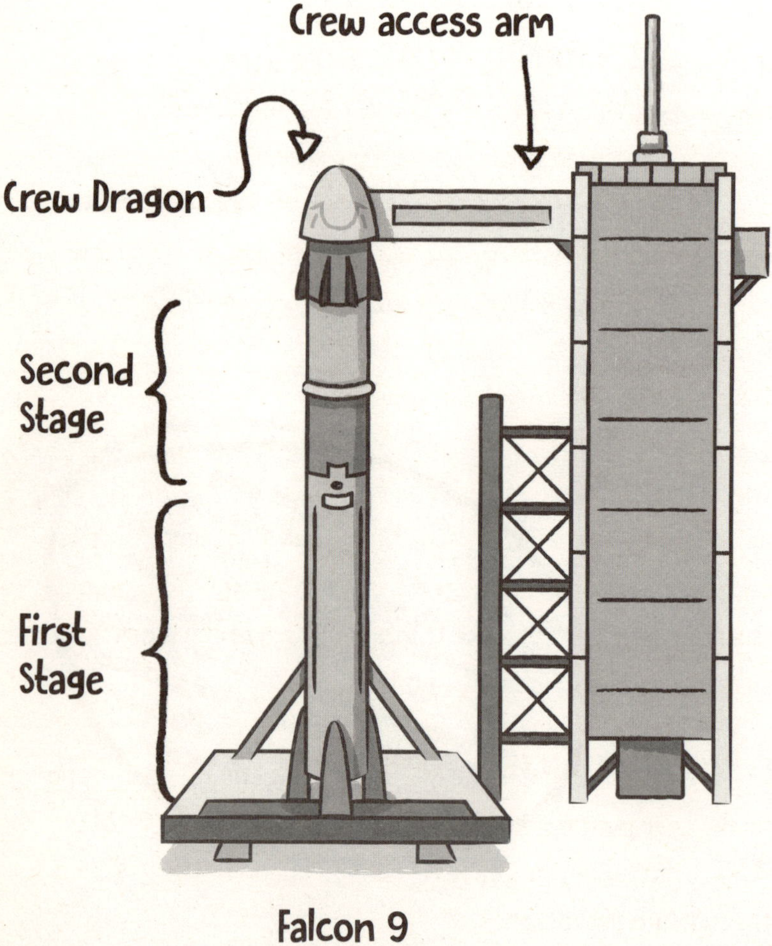

Crew access arm

Crew Dragon

Second Stage

First Stage

Falcon 9
Spacecraft

L-minus 2 hours 15 minutes: We did the ingress (a fancy word for saying we got into the Dragon) and settled into our seats, which were moulded to each of our bodies. It felt so comfy in there, cocooned in a seat made specially for me – and actually pretty roomy, too! We stashed Dougie in his crate right behind us.

L-minus 1 hour 50 minutes: Our closeout crew from the space agency did our seatbelts up for us, plugged in our "umbilical cords", and made sure we were comfortable. They also helped me hang a soft toy, Paxi, from the ceiling above on a piece of string. It's an old astronaut trick to show a crew when they've reached space. A toy suspended on a string will start floating as soon as the spacecraft enters microgravity. It's not exactly techy but it IS super cute!

Then, once the crew had left and closed the hatch behind them, our seats reclined so Mum (the commander) and Dad (the pilot) could see the three touchscreens above them that they would use to help fly us to the ISS. I started getting excited, but Dad said we still had a long wait.

L-minus 45 minutes: The Launch Director on the ground finally gave permission for **"Go"**. But it still wasn't **actual "Go"** – not quite yet. This was just a go ahead to start loading the fuel into the rocket.

L-minus 1 minute: Mum and Dad did the final prelaunch computer checks. (Now I could get excited!)

L-minus 45 seconds: The Launch Director said, "Go for launch." (*REALLY* excited!!!)

L-minus 3 seconds: The engine ignited, and...

LIFT OFF!!!

The best way I can describe the feeling of blasting into space is like the most intense rollercoaster you've ever been on, but without any loop-the-loops. As fuel is used up, the rocket gets lighter and it goes faster, and the more you get pressed back into your seat. That made me feel safe though, like the seat was giving my body a big, tight hug.

There were big jolts and bangs now and again as each stage of the rocket detached. Every jolt thrust my body forwards briefly against the safety straps, and then... Paxi started twirling around like a small cuddly ballerina above my head.

The invisible hand pressing me back into my seat disappeared, and I realised my arms were now floating up towards my head. I had to concentrate super hard to hold them down against my body. We were in orbit! We were in microgravity! And **that,** dearest diary, feels better than any rollercoaster in the world. ☺

I've got to go and have my breakfast now, but I'll be back later to share the results of my next assignment for Ms Asimov. Mum's helping me with this one in exchange for me making her morning coffee for a week. Hope I can remember how to work the espresso machine!

11:30 am

Okay, coffee machines are really complicated – even ones made by space agencies specifically for operating in microgravity. Mum said it tasted great though and way better than when Dad makes it. 😊

So, Andromeda's Assignment Number Two is... to interview an astronaut. Good job I'm on the ISS!

I chose Mum, as she's flown on a couple of missions before this one and has been a commander as well as a flight engineer.

She's totally awesome.

ASSIGNMENT NUMBER TWO

INTERVIEW WITH ASTRONAUT KATHRYN JANE FUTURA

. . . .

by Andromeda Futura, Astronaut-in-Training (hopefully)

AF: Astronaut Futura, how did you get to space on your first mission?

KF: Well, it was a few years ago now, but I first came to the ISS in a Soyuz spacecraft, which is smaller than a Dragon and only fits three crew members inside. There are no touchscreens in a Soyuz. Instead, there's a panel with *hundreds* of different switches and buttons. I'm short, so I needed an extendable stick to reach the buttons higher up on the panel! I loved it though – there's something satisfying about flipping switches and pressing buttons to fly a spacecraft!

AF: What was your Launch Day like?

KF: I remember waking up and thinking, "Today I woke up on Earth, and I'll fall asleep in space". That blew my mind. We had to clean our bodies really thoroughly, and I made sure I took my time in the shower, as it would be the last time I'd feel water running through my hair for a while! The rest of the day went quite like ours did – eating a meal that wouldn't come back up if we got space sickness, suiting up, and travelling to our rocket.

AF: What was it like to be in a crew that's not your family?
KF: I had such great crewmates that they almost felt like family! I'd been training for 3½ years for my first mission, and I got to know them really well during that time. You have to be a really close team as a crew, and there were plenty of fun things we did together as well as the training, like creating our expedition poster.

AF: The expedition poster! I loved doing ours!
KF: Me too! It's my favourite space agency tradition – creating a poster from a photo of the crew for each new expedition. A while ago, instead of having a regular photo in flight suits, one crew dressed up in costumes and recreated a movie poster for theirs.

AF: What's your biggest tip for life on the space station?
KF: Hook-and-loop tape! Fix a patch of hook-and-loop tape to everything you've brought up with you, and then you can stick your belongings to any one of the patches that are already attached to all the flat surfaces up here. And, if you really want to have some fun, you could stick hook-and-loop tape to the soles of your shoes, step from patch to patch on the surfaces, and pretend you can walk in space!

AF: And one final question... Can I do an EVA?
KF: Absolutely not, Andromeda. It's FAR too dangerous. And don't go asking your Dad – the answer will still be no!

Hmmm. Looks like I've got some work to do before I can make my chosen mission happen. There's plenty of time though – and I can be prettttttty persuasive.

Okay diary, I'm off to see what Perri's up to. He'll either be eating, working out, or looking at himself in the mirror. Talk to you later!

CHAPTER THREE

2:00 pm
- - - - - -

So, Douglas has a new BFF. I'd be jealous, except she's made from metal and sensors **and** a whole bunch of other super high-tech components. He sniffed her out this morning and now I can't get him to leave her side – which is why I am writing in you, dear diary, from the Destiny lab where I have now been for approximately **FOUR HOURS**.

You see, my daft old mutt has fallen in love with a robot dog. She's got eyes, ears, a tail, and legs. She can even wiggle her bum. Her South Korean designer back on Earth, Jihee Kim, named her Laïka, which is super cool, because the IRL Laïka was a dog sent into space by Russia in 1957.

That Laïka was the first living creature to orbit Earth. Douglas just knows this Laïka as "fwend who must be played with for infinity".

I mean, I'm pretending to be grumpy about all of this. But, actually, the robots on the International Space Station are literally **THE coolest thing** up here, and I've had an absolute ball (no, Dougie, not a tennis ball) hanging out in this module today. The astronauts have let me observe the robots like a real scientist would and have told me loads about them and why they are so important for future missions further into space.* I wonder if I can study robotics... is it a class I can take at school when we get back to Earth? I'll ask Mum and Dad later.

For now, though, let me take you to meet our ISS robots.

*Which was ALSO helpful because Deep Space is precisely the topic of my next Ms Asimov assignment. ☺ More on that later...

Made of **titanium**, a light but strong metal that will withstand severe conditions, especially when travelling further into space

ECG sensors in the places where an astronaut might pet Laïka that can check their pulse rate or blood pressure and other vital signs of health

A **handle** to carry equipment or to help an astronaut carry Laïka!

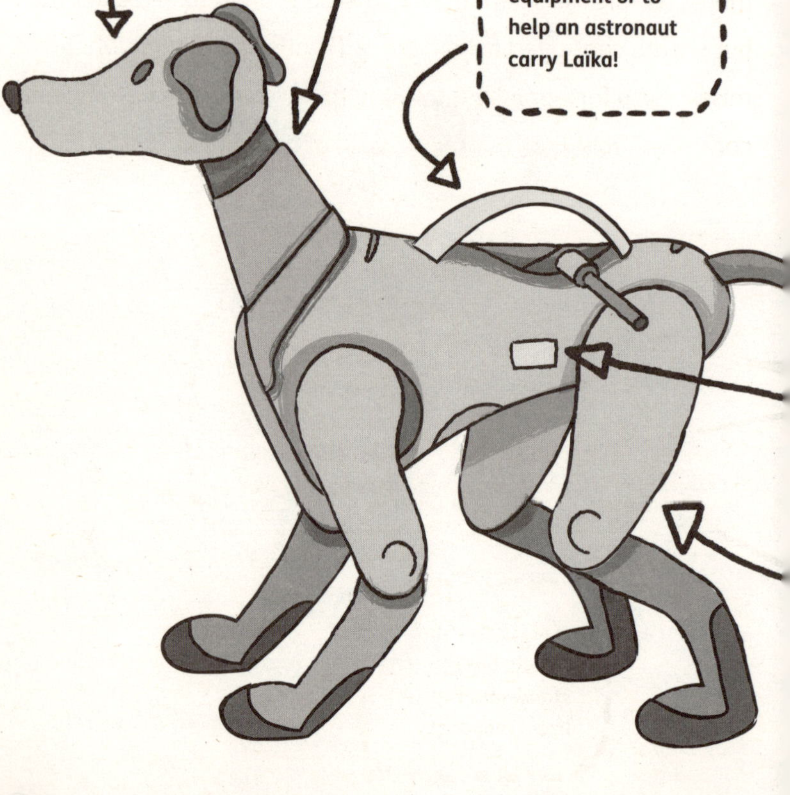

LAïKA

First up is robodog Laïka, who was designed to be an Artificial Intelligence (AI) companion for astronauts going on really long missions to Mars or the moon. It's important that she looks and moves like a real dog, because she can help astronauts feel less alone and disconnected from the world they've left behind.

There are other robot dogs, like Bert. Bert has legs that are designed to help him crawl into caves or climb up hills on the moon or Mars. He's kept at DLR, the German Aerospace Centre, but can be controlled from the ISS. (That's practice for when missions go further into space and robots can be more efficiently controlled from Earth's orbit instead of back on Earth itself.)

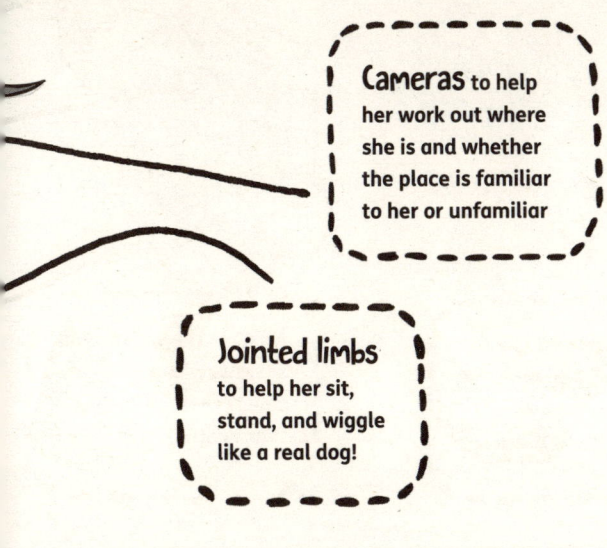

Cameras to help her work out where she is and whether the place is familiar to her or unfamiliar

Jointed limbs to help her sit, stand, and wiggle like a real dog!

BUMBLE, HONEY, and QUEEN

From robodogs to robobees! This trio of flying robots are the Astrobees, and they spend their time buzzing around the ISS doing basic jobs – like moving cargo or monitoring air quality – so astronauts don't have to. They can even find lost things! (Just ask Perri. He **NEVER** remembers to stick his stuff down...)

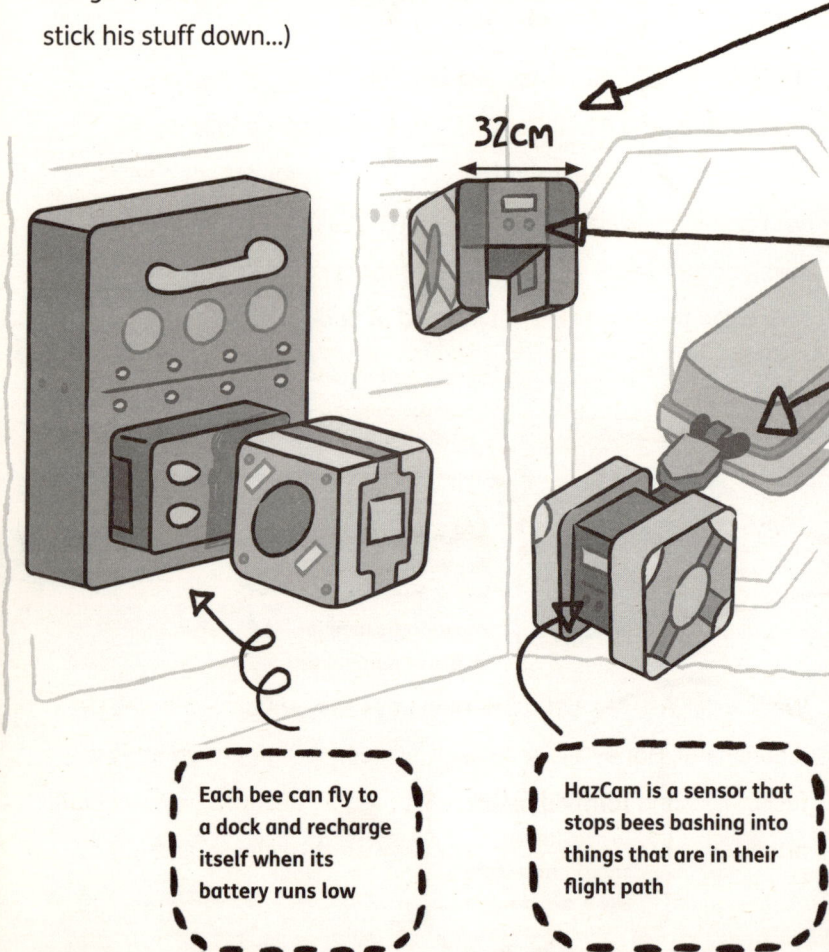

32cm

Each bee can fly to a dock and recharge itself when its battery runs low

HazCam is a sensor that stops bees bashing into things that are in their flight path

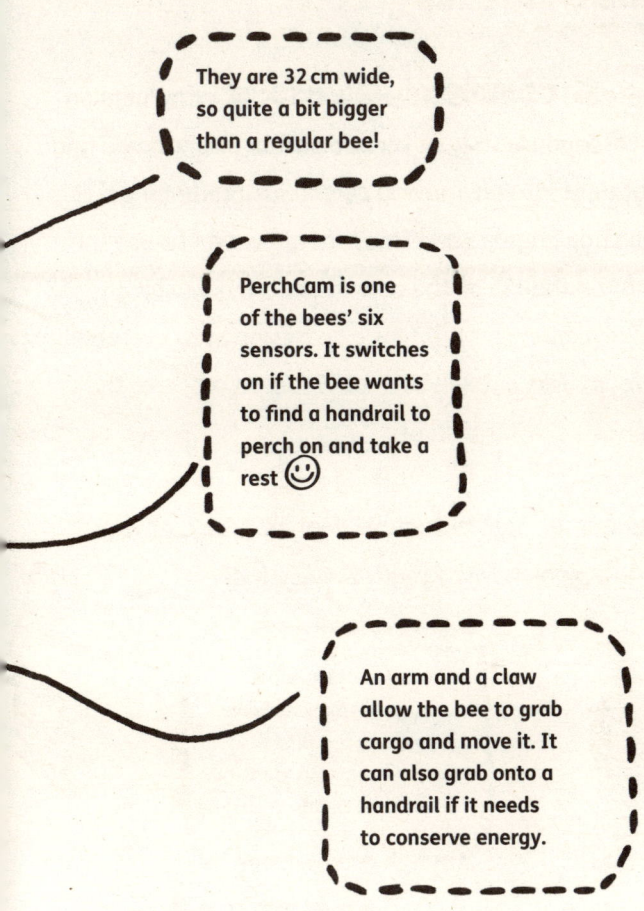

They are 32 cm wide, so quite a bit bigger than a regular bee!

PerchCam is one of the bees' six sensors. It switches on if the bee wants to find a handrail to perch on and take a rest 😊

An arm and a claw allow the bee to grab cargo and move it. It can also grab onto a handrail if it needs to conserve energy.

We tell our Astrobee buddies apart by their colours – Bumble has a blue shell, Honey's is yellow, and Queen's is green. Douglas is fascinated and terrified by them – probably because he can't work out if *he* wants to chase *them* or *they* want to chase *him*! 😊

HUMANOIDS

Humanoid robots are **completely awesome** as helpers on Earth or in space, because they're shaped sort of like humans and designed to slot right into environments already made for us. This space humanoid has fingers and arms that allow him to use the same equipment on the ISS as the astronauts – e.g. pushing buttons or flipping switches – but he's also designed to eventually take on dangerous tasks outside of the ISS too, to preserve the astronauts' precious time and safety.

So, diary – meet our resident humanoid, Marvin. (You'd never guess my favourite book is *Hitchhiker's Guide...* 😊)

> If you touch Marvin's arm, he'll stop whatever he's doing thanks to sensors that can identify a human's touch

> His legs are verrrrrry long and jointed in seven places to help him get around the ISS*

* I've seen Marvin's moves – a high-tech, two-legged octopus comes to mind! 😊

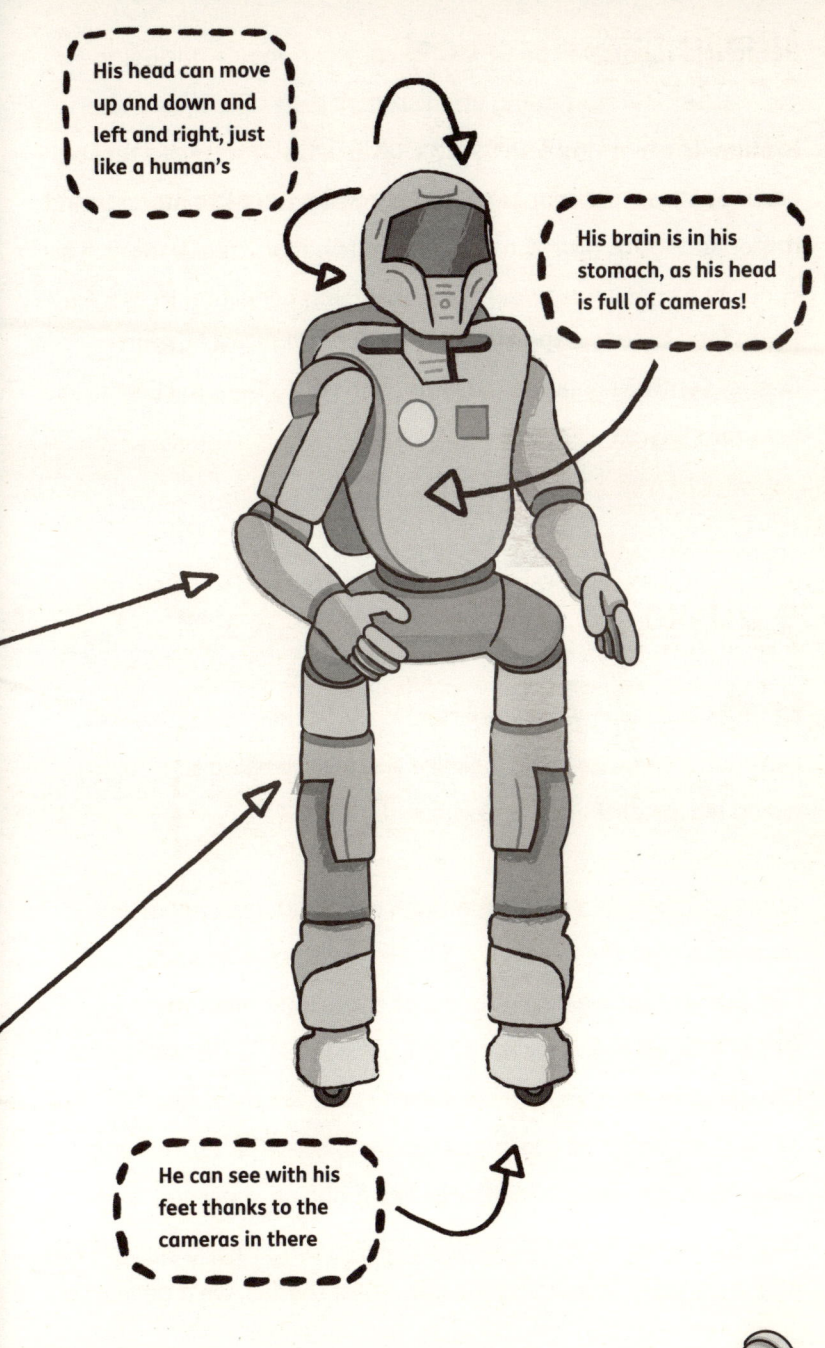

Humanoid robots will be **crucial** once astronauts (including me – hopefully) start going on missions deeper into space, like to Mars. The humans won't stay forever, so who will keep those bases spotless and running smoothly when the astronauts aren't there? Robots, of course.

I wonder if there's a spare Marvin kicking around at Mission Control Centre? I need all the help I can get to keep my Earth bedroom tidy.

4:00 pm

Finally back in my crew quarters now. I convinced one of the astronauts to make Laïka look like she was sleeping so Douglas would leave her there and come with me.

Today has definitely made me think lots about how important robotics are on the ISS, as it's not just creature-bots and humanoids that we have around us here. Remember the **gigantic arms** attached to the outside of the ISS that I told you about before? They're not exactly cute like the Astrobees, but we rely on these enormous robots to keep the ISS running properly. If we couldn't do things like grabbing spacecraft arriving from Earth or moving astronauts around when they're out doing an EVA, or even inspecting the outside of the ISS, we'd be in a bit of a pickle. And Dad gets all excited when it's his turn to operate one of the arms from inside, which is cute and makes me happy.

Anyway, time to write up my assignment now. Ms Asimov asked me to research robotics in Deep Space – i.e. the parts of space far beyond the Earth's atmosphere – and send her my favourite factoids. ("Without bothering the crew, Andromeda!")

So, presenting the results of my research. (Sorry, Ms A, I *did* bother the crew, and they were **totally happy** about it. Turns out even grown-up astronauts are like big kids when it comes to talking about Mars!) **Prepare to be amazed and astounded!**

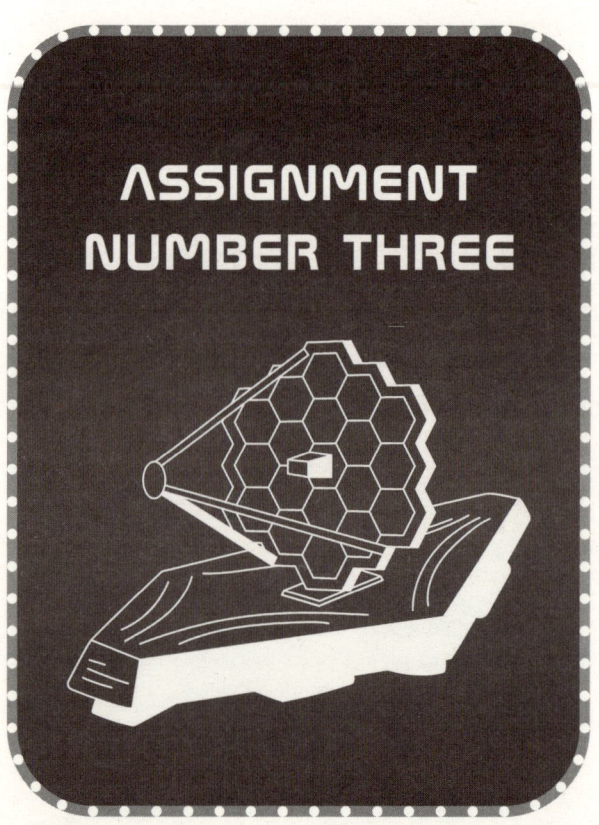

ASSIGNMENT NUMBER THREE

ANDI'S RIVETING
RESEARCH
REVELATIONS

(Deep Space Edition)

Rosalind Franklin Rover

Even though this sounds like a robot dog (Rover – get it?!), it's actually a **robotic vehicle**. Its mission is to look for signs of water and life on the Red Planet from the past and present in an area where scientists think there was once an ancient ocean. It can drill down to depths of up to 2 metres below the surface to collect a sample (the deepest ever) and then transfer it into its own belly, where an onboard laboratory can do analysis and send the results back to scientists on Earth. For a planet where a human would die in so many different gruesome ways if they weren't wearing a spacesuit (e.g. your blood would boil – gross), sending a robot to do the science first seems like a pretty sensible idea to me...

I also **LOVE** how the rover is named after Rosalind Franklin, a scientist who did pioneering work on DNA (a chemical found inside every single cell of every single living thing). She helped us to understand what a life is made from, just like the rover's mission is to look for life on Mars. **Awesome!**

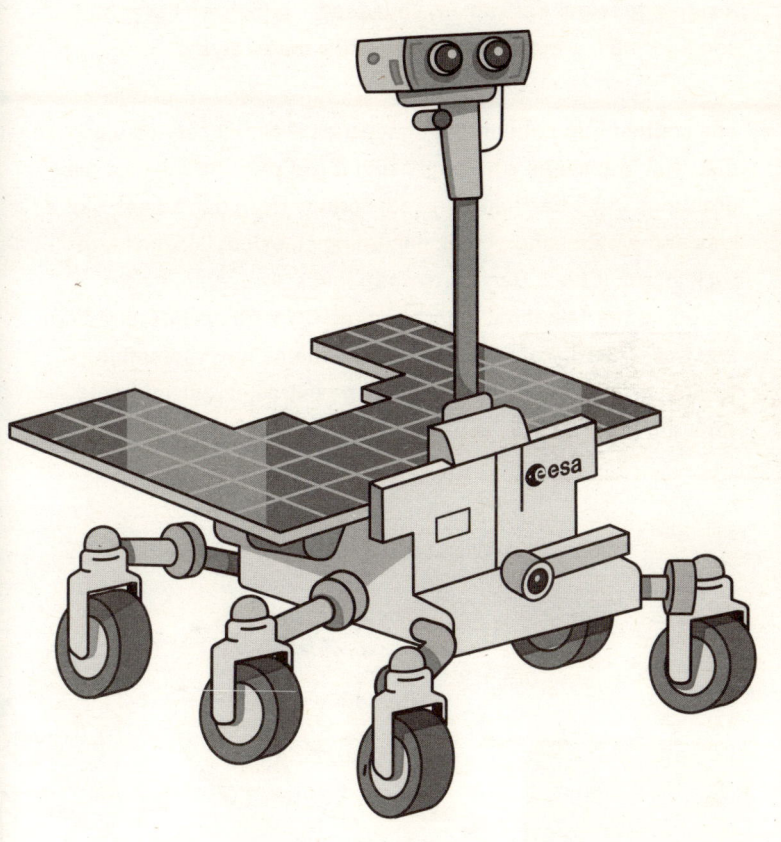

Voyager 1

This robotic probe, launched back in Ancient Times (i.e. 1977), is the human-made object furthest from Earth. It takes a day for a signal to reach Earth from Voyager 1 – which isn't that bad, considering it's more than **15 BILLION miles away!**

The coolest thing about this spacecraft is that it carries a golden disc that any aliens who might find it can play. On the disc are greetings in 55 Earth languages; sounds from our planet, like a kiss and whale song; music, including classical (Mozart) and rock 'n' roll (Chuck Berry – my nan loves him); and images including the Taj Mahal in India, some Olympic sprinters racing, and the structure of DNA (in case the aliens have something similar in their cells). It's basically an extra-terrestrial time capsule. 🙂

Webb Space Telescope

This mighty telescope orbits the sun and sends incredible images more than 1,500,000 km to Earth to help scientists understand the history of the Universe – including how our Solar System formed. To be honest, the science boggles my brain a little, as what the telescope is doing is basically looking back in time to when galaxies were young! Because – as far as science knows – nothing can move faster than the speed of light. And the galaxies are so far away that the light from them takes a **very, very, VERY** long time (i.e. billions of years) to travel to the telescope. So the images collected by Webb and sent to earth are of those galaxies when they were just babies! **Mind. Blown.**

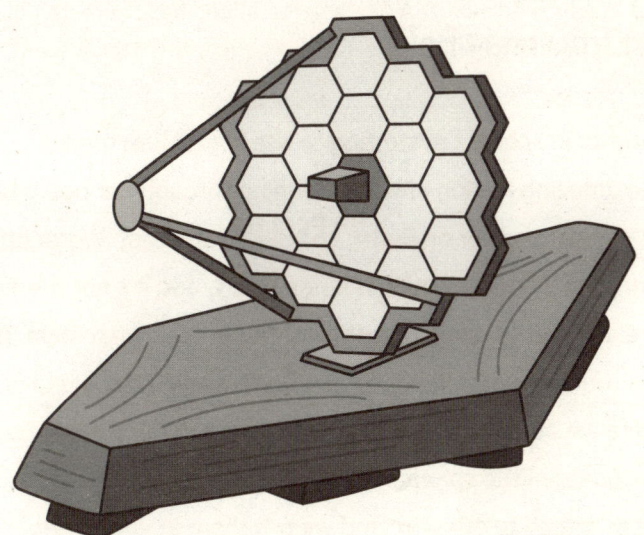

I wonder if the telescope has ever observed the Andromeda constellation? Definitely need to ask Ms Asimov next time we video chat.

CHAPTER FOUR

8:00 am

It's Towel Day! (AKA The Best Day of the Week.) Every Sunday, we change over our used towels for fresh, clean ones. There's no washing machine up here, so all the towels we'll need for the mission have to come from Earth, and we have a strict changeover day once a week so we don't end up running out of clean ones!

Ick. Can you imagine?

After a month in space, I'm starting to see what Mum meant about the amazing feeling of water running through her hair when she took her last shower on Earth. I **REALLY** miss that. Water on the International Space Station is kinda sticky, and it's not running anywhere! Not out of a tap, or a shower head, or down a drain. If there *was* running water, it would just float away in blobs and go everywhere we don't want it to (like into computers). Instead, we carefully squeeze little spheres of it from special pouches which then sort of attach to our skin, and we rub them in.

Dad told me that keeping clean on the ISS is more like how he and Mum used to keep clean at the music festivals they went to when

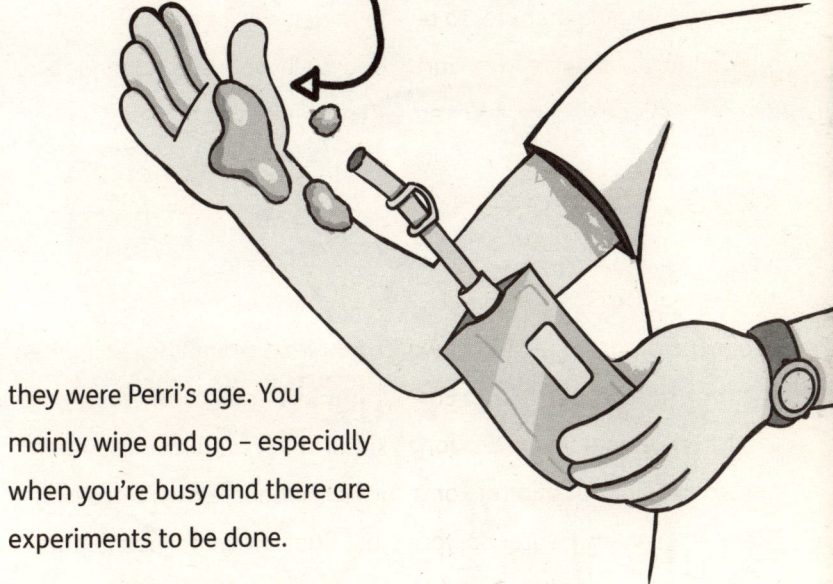

Water forms spherical blobs in space, because there's barely any gravity to exert force and pull its molecules apart. Up here, the molecules can cling really tightly together and form the shape with the smallest surface area on the outside – the sphere!

they were Perri's age. You mainly wipe and go – especially when you're busy and there are experiments to be done.

Hey, diary – I've just had a brainwave.

Come with me and my new towels to Hygiene Corner, and I will tell you more there. Ms Asimov's given me the weekend to describe my space hygiene routine, so I can complete my fourth assignment at the same time.

8:55 am

Okay, so I'm in Hygiene Corner now. I had to wait a bit (actually, **AGES**) for Perri to be done in there first. He said he was clipping his toenails. **Gross**. Anyway, Hygiene Corner isn't like a proper bathroom – it's literally a small corner of the ISS with a curtain you can pull across for some privacy. I like to sing when I'm in there to make doubly sure no one will come in. ☺

ASSIGNMENT NUMBER FOUR

How to shower

There are a few things you need to bring with you for an ISS "shower":

Towels – These aren't the soft, fluffy kind of towels you might find in a ballroom on Earth. That would take up way too much room on a very full space station! Space towels are thin but really absorbent, and the washcloths are condensed into tiny little pellets that you unwrap. At least with the washcloths you get a new one every other day.

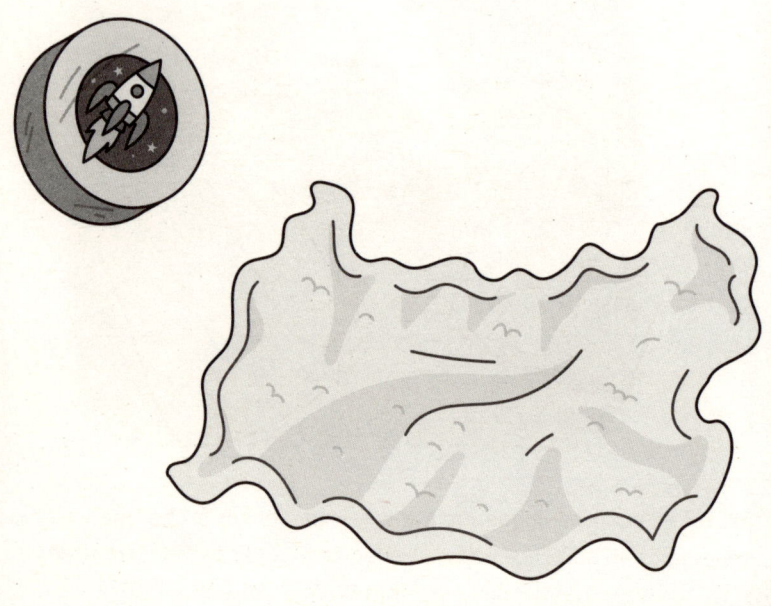

Soap – Sadly, there are no scented bottles of luxury shower gel on offer up here. If there were, you might end up smelling lovely but dealing with a Really Big Problem, as soap bubbles floating away and getting into the electronics would be **CATASTROPHIC!** Instead, we have a pouch containing powdered soap that we add water to. One of these pouches has to last two weeks, so we've got to be careful when we squirt that stuff out!

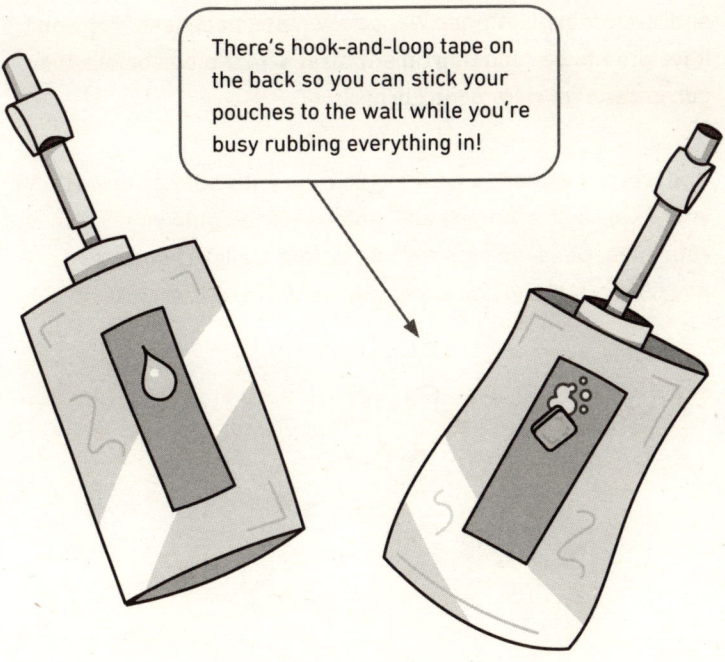

There's hook-and-loop tape on the back so you can stick your pouches to the wall while you're busy rubbing everything in!

Water – I've already been to the water dispenser in the Destiny module to fill my water pouch with warm water for my "shower". (You can choose cold water too, but WHY WOULD YOU?!!)

So, when you've got all your kit ready, you either squirt your soap and your water blobs straight onto your skin and rub it in. **OR** you squirt them into your washcloth and rub that on your skin instead! If, like today, it's **Self Care Sunday** and you're taking your time with a long leisurely "shower", then the first method is great. But if you're in a rush because you've got five minutes before you have to speak to Mission Control Centre, or take a reading from an experiment, or finish an assignment for your favourite teacher in the whole world 😊, then the squirt-on-washcloth-quick-wipedown option is best. You won't have time to be rounding up any stray water blobs before they can escape from Hygiene Corner!

And when it comes to washing your hair, it's similar to washing your skin. Just shampoo and water squirted onto your scalp and rubbed in. Good job I cut my hair before we left! I only need a tiny bit of shampoo and water now, and it takes way less time. 😊

How to clean your teeth

Spoiler: There's no special high-tech space toothbrush or toothpaste for making your smile sparkle! Just a regular old brush and toothpaste like back on Earth. To clean your teeth in microgravity, you:

1. Squirt a blob of water onto your brush. It'll sink into the bristles.

2. Suck the blob of water from the brush into your mouth and swallow it. Your brush will still be left nice and wet.

3. Squirt toothpaste onto your wet brush. The toothpaste will be sort of sticky, so don't worry about it floating away and going up your nose or anything.

4. Brush! (Don't forget the ones at the back!)

5. Swallow the toothpaste. (Or spit it into your towel. Both are pretty gross, but remember – there's no sink or running water up here. ☺)

How to keep yourself tidy

You definitely can't have long nails in space. They'd only get in the way of experiments using your hands. Plus, the thought of snagging one in a spacesuit glove makes me wince. Just keep them short and tidy.

The best way to clip your nails is to do it over one of the many ventilation grids that are part of the air circulation system on the ISS. Your clippings will be pulled towards the grid, and you can vacuum them up later.*

* Same goes for hair and vacuum cleaners. Funnily enough we can't just fly a barber up here, so astronauts use clippers attached to a vacuum cleaner for suction. Sometimes we'll cut each other's hair, although Perri has banned me from going anywhere near his fade. Probably because he knows I'd shave a heart into it or something.

How to go to the toilet

Every single kid in my class had questions about this before I left for space. Class 7B – this one's for you!

Q: How does a space toilet work?
A: It's in two parts. The first part is a tube with a bright yellow funnel and suction. You pee into the funnel and the urine gets sucked away so blobs of it don't end up floating around the ISS and hitting your fellow astronauts in the face. Bleurgh. For a poo, you use foot- and hand-holds to position yourself over a silver canister with a little seat and a hole that you have to … err… aim into. 😊 There's also suction here. (For the same reason you don't want floating blobs of pee… I don't have to spell this one out, right?) Inside the canister is a bag that collects the poo, which is then sealed and compacted. It's good space manners to put a fresh bag in for the next person.

Q: What if you don't get your aim right?!
A: There're always wet wipes, but we actually did lots of training in how to go to the toilet in space before we left Earth! For poo practice, you put a little sticker on your bum and you have to position yourself over the seat hole in a pretend toilet with a camera beneath the seat. There's a screen in front of you connected to the camera, so you can see if your sticker is in the right position or not!

Q: In space, can everyone hear you pee?

A: The daily business of a working space station is so noisy that there's no way anyone can hear you peeing. (Or doing a poo for that matter!) Unless they had their ear right up to the privacy curtain, which would just be weird.

Q: Do you use toilet paper?

A: Yes! We get a choice, as it happens. I like extra soft.

Q: What happens to all the waste?

A: The poo canisters get stored away until they can be burned up in a return cargo vehicle, although sometimes astronaut poo goes back to Earth to be studied. Pee – I hope you're ready for this – gets cleaned, treated, and then turned into drinking water! Yep. Astronauts drink their own pee. 🙂 (I'm going to tell you much more about this once I've had a chance to properly investigate the Water Recovery System on board. No one's had time to teach me yet!)

That concludes Andi's tour of Hygiene Corner. I hope you enjoyed your visit. Please rate and review. 🙂 (That means you, Ms Asimov! Five stars, right?)

1:00 pm

I think I just swallowed one of Perri's floating toenail clippings... **HE FORGOT THE SUCTION – AGAIN!**

CHAPTER FIVE

6:00 am

- - - - - - -

Ugh, why hasn't anyone invented breath freshener for dogs?! Douglas woke me up this morning with a gross, sloppy lick right across my face. He definitely needs to be more chill.

What can I do to tire him out? Back on Earth, he would chase sticks (and squirrels, and leaves, and other dogs) for hours in the park. No park on the International Space Station, though, and I'm 99.9% sure there are no trees either. **HANG ON!** What about Mum's big experiment? She definitely mentioned plants. Or was it a space garden? I'm sure she said something about growing food in space. Anyway, whatever it is, maybe there's a stick in there I can borrow for Dougie, and I can sneak a peek at her experiment while I'm there, too.

Okay, I can hear Dad's still shuffling about in his sleeping compartment, and I think that's Mum singing while she space-showers. This is my chance, dear diary. If you want me, I'll be in the lab. ☺

2:00 pm
— — — — —

Sooooo. No sticks. (Sorry, Douglas.) AND – **OOPS** – Mum caught me snooping around. But the good news is that she needs a lab partner today anyway, and Dad's had to talk to Mission Control Centre about something lonnnng and boring, so **GUESS WHO GETS TO DO AN ACTUAL EXPERIMENT, LIKE AN ACTUAL REAL-LIFE ASTRONAUT????!** ☺ I think Ms Asimov is going to be so impressed with my next assignment...

ASSIGNMENT NUMBER FIVE

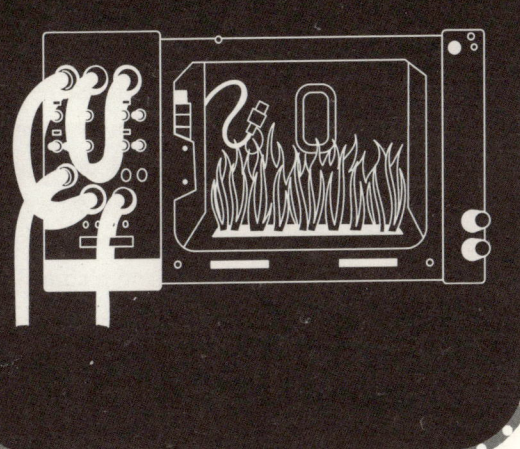

BOTANY EXPERIMENT

By Andromeda Futura, Apprentice Astronaut

How to be a Space Farmer

What's the botanical problem to solve?

Astronauts only get food deliveries every couple of months when resupply missions are sent from Earth.* BUT, what about when we start going on missions that take us deeper into space and further from our planet, like to Mars? There'll be no resupply rockets coming back and forth to top us up then, and we could be out there for YEARS at a time! Nutrients in food that keep our bodies healthy can start to break down, even in the vacuum-packed space food we eat up here, so we'll need fresh plants that can feed us and keep our bodies in tip-top mission condition. And that's where Space Farmers come in.

*Ms Asimov – someone at Mission Control Centre really needs to tell Perri. He's DEFINITELY having too many second helpings.

But what's so amazing about plants?

Ermmmm... lots! On Earth, plants absorb the carbon dioxide we breathe out and create oxygen that we breathe in. On the ISS, carbon dioxide is removed by chemical reaction, but oxygen's a bit different. Some of our supply is delivered by the resupply missions, and some we make ourselves through hydrolysis of water – where water molecules get broken up and the oxygen gas released using an electric current.

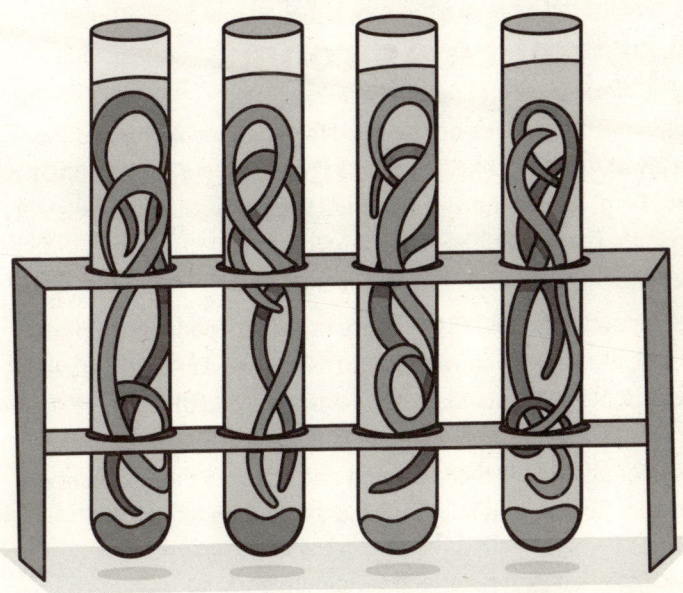

But what's even more amazing is a microorganism called **SPIRULINA** that could make life a whole lot easier for astronauts. (Technically it's neither an algae, nor a plant, as it doesn't have roots – but it's green and definitely looks like a forest when it's growing under the ocean.) In tests on Earth, it's been great at absorbing the CO_2 that we breathe out and converting it back into oxygen. It's also got more protein per gram than any other food on Earth, as well as loads of vitamins, minerals, and other important things that our bodies need, like antioxidants.

AND spirulina grows really easily and looks like it can handle very high levels of cosmic radiation without its cells going all weird and mutating into something too unhealthy for humans to eat. At the top, its growth is not impacted by weightlessness, as demonstrated on board the ISS. It's an actual **SUPERfood**!

So is there an actual Space Farm?
Yes! Kind of... and it's on the ISS. It's called the **Advanced Plant Habitat (APH)**. It's like an uber fancy greenhouse with **LOADS** of cool tech, but it's the size of a mini fridge, because, surprisingly enough, space stations really aren't that big!

Astronauts use the APH to figure out what conditions different plants like to grow in when they're in space. On Earth, gravity helps a plant's roots to grow downwards and their stems to grow upwards. Studying plants in our mini–Space Farm can tell us a lot about how they respond and adapt to the microgravity up here so they can still grow big and strong.

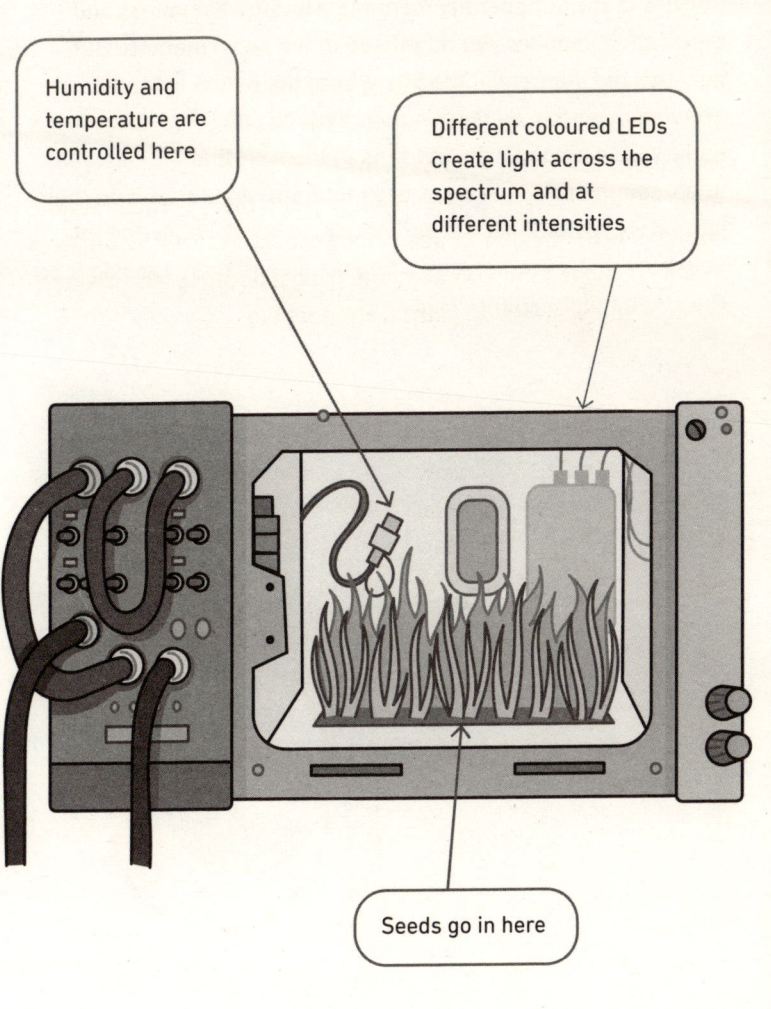

Humidity and temperature are controlled here

Different coloured LEDs create light across the spectrum and at different intensities

Seeds go in here

And what's growing in the APH today?

Mum started with chilli pepper seeds that have grown into flowers that will hopefully turn into fruit (the actual red and green chilli peppers you might see in the supermarket). But because the stamens – the bits where the pollen is found – are growing upwards, as there's no gravity to pull them down like there would be on Earth, the fans in the APH that are designed to spread the pollen like a breeze on Earth would can't do their job. So we're doing all the pollination by hand; collecting the pollen from the stamens on a tiny brush and then dabbing it on the stigma of the plant.

Chilli peppers are great because they contain more vitamin C than an orange.

And in case you don't like chilli peppers, astronauts have already grown a whole veggie aisle of crops in their space-salad experiments: lettuces, radishes, cabbages, kale, pak choi **AND** some pretty flowers called zinnias, right in time for Valentine's Day (although, best not to eat your Valentine's bouquet).

Astronauts get poor drainage in their sinuses (gross!) which means it's harder to smell and taste food. Some chunks of chilli in our meals will help to cut through those blocked sinuses and make food way more flavourful.

SPACE CR

Research into crops in space might also help farmers on Earth with growing crops in challenging environments.

Scientists have successfully grown plants in samples of moon dust brought back from the moon by the Apollo 11, 12, and 17 astronauts in the 1960s and 1970s!

5:00 pm

Mum said that the most amazing thing plants can do in space is help astronauts feel connected to Earth, and that definitely helps when you're hanging out more than 400 km above all your friends. She looked a bit sad when she said it, so we sniffed a few leaves and gave some of the plants a drink. I think she felt better afterwards. (I definitely did. It made me think of Nan's veggie patch back on Earth.) Anyway, Mum's promised I can keep helping her with the chilli pepper experiment as long as I do my assignments on time, keep my crew quarters tidy, and don't bother my brother. Just wait till Ms Asimov reads my botany report! I bet she'll show it to all the top people at Mission Control Centre and they'll all be putting spirulina in their breakfast smoothies before we know it.

Oh! Gotta go – Dougie's got loose from his straps **AGAIN** and he's on his way to the Cupola...

CHAPTER SIX

5:00 pm

I can't believe I have agreed to this, diary, but... **I'm about to go and work out with Perri.** Yep, my big brother who, back on Earth, can normally be found at the squat rack (or flexing his muscles in the mirror) – has decided I need some help with my workouts. He's taken it upon himself to be my personal trainer. Which basically means he's going to beast me. I'm totally up for whatever he suggests – just as long as he doesn't make me drink one of his **disgusting** protein shakes afterwards.

The thing is, it might actually be quite good to work out with Perri's help. Why? Well, **a)** we have to do two hours of exercise a day while we're up here, and that's a lonnnnnng time (although we can watch movies and box sets we've downloaded to our devices while we train, so it's not all bad). And **b)** my new assignment from Ms Asimov is to write a fitness programme for an astronaut, so this is perfect timing. ☺

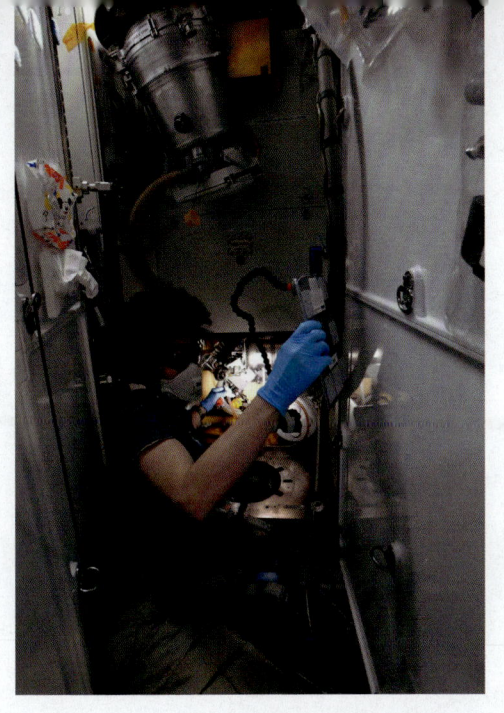

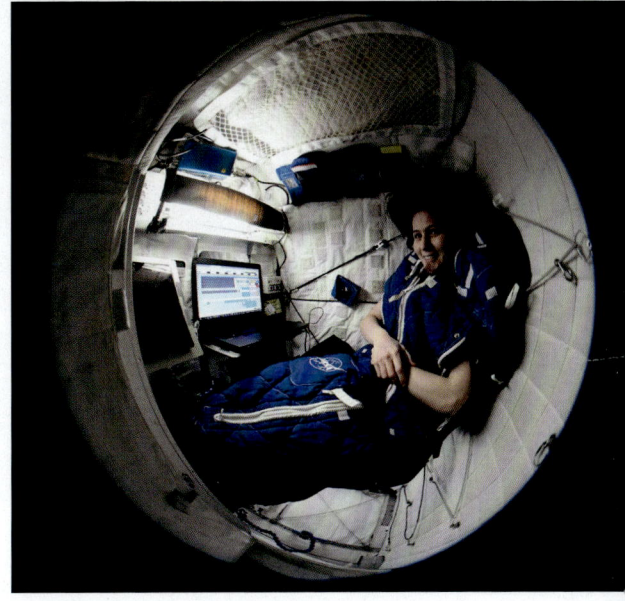

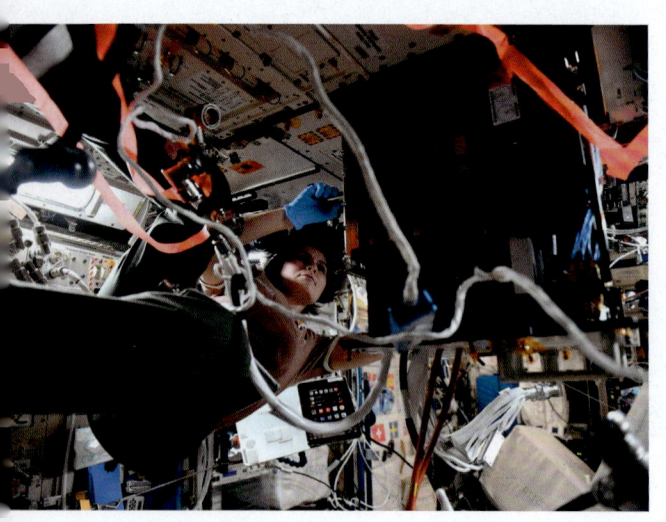

I mean, I **LOVE** sports back on Earth. I'm in athletics club at school, and I do gymnastics training, and I swim twice a week. And I walk Douglas every day after I've finished my homework. But up here on the International Space Station, exercise isn't just for fun or to stay healthy or be part of a team. It's to stop our bones and muscles from weakening and wasting away. Yep – it's really, really, REALLY important to do.

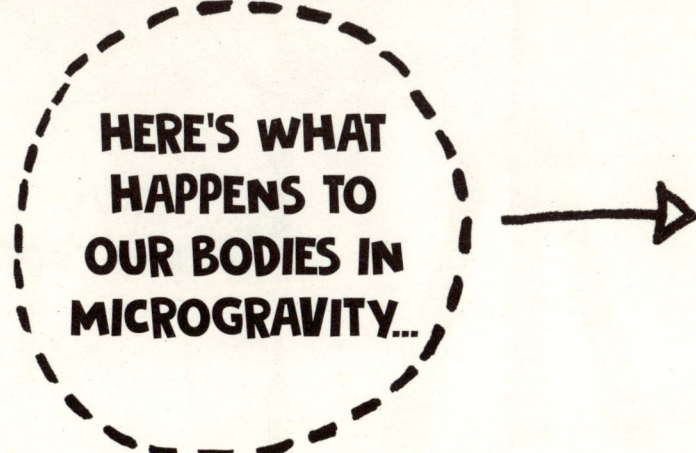

HERE'S WHAT HAPPENS TO OUR BODIES IN MICROGRAVITY...

→

Earth

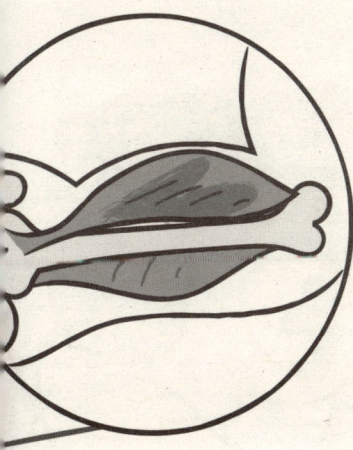

On Earth, our bones and muscles are constantly working hard against the force of gravity – even just to keep us standing upright!

Muscles are attached to bones and apply force to the bones when they move. The stronger the muscles, the more force is applied

Bones stay strong by working hard, because new bone cells form when force is applied to them

In space, our bones and muscles aren't fighting against gravity to support our body weight

Bone cells will stop forming and bones will become less dense if they don't have force applied to them

Muscles will get smaller and weaker if they're not working hard

Luckily, we have some cool kit on the ISS to help us keep our bones dense and our muscles flexing. (Which all helps to make sure we don't break when we go back to Earth!) There's the...

Treadmill

It looks a little like the treadmills you might find in a gym on Earth, but here in space we don't have our weight pulling our bodies down to the ground. Instead, we use a system of clip-on bungees and a harness to recreate the sensation of being pulled downwards. I got weird pins and needles in the soles of my feet when I first started running on the ISS treadmill. (It's because we don't use our feet much up here, and so they forget what it feels like to have the full force of body weight pushing down on them.) I'm much more used to it now, though.

Mum even ran a whole marathon on the ISS treadmill while she was here on her first mission, at the exact same time as the real race was happening on Earth! That's 42.195 km! (If you haven't realised already, diary – my mum's a total badass.)

A bar to grab for balance and to pull yourself up once the bungees are clipped in – I needed it all the time to start with

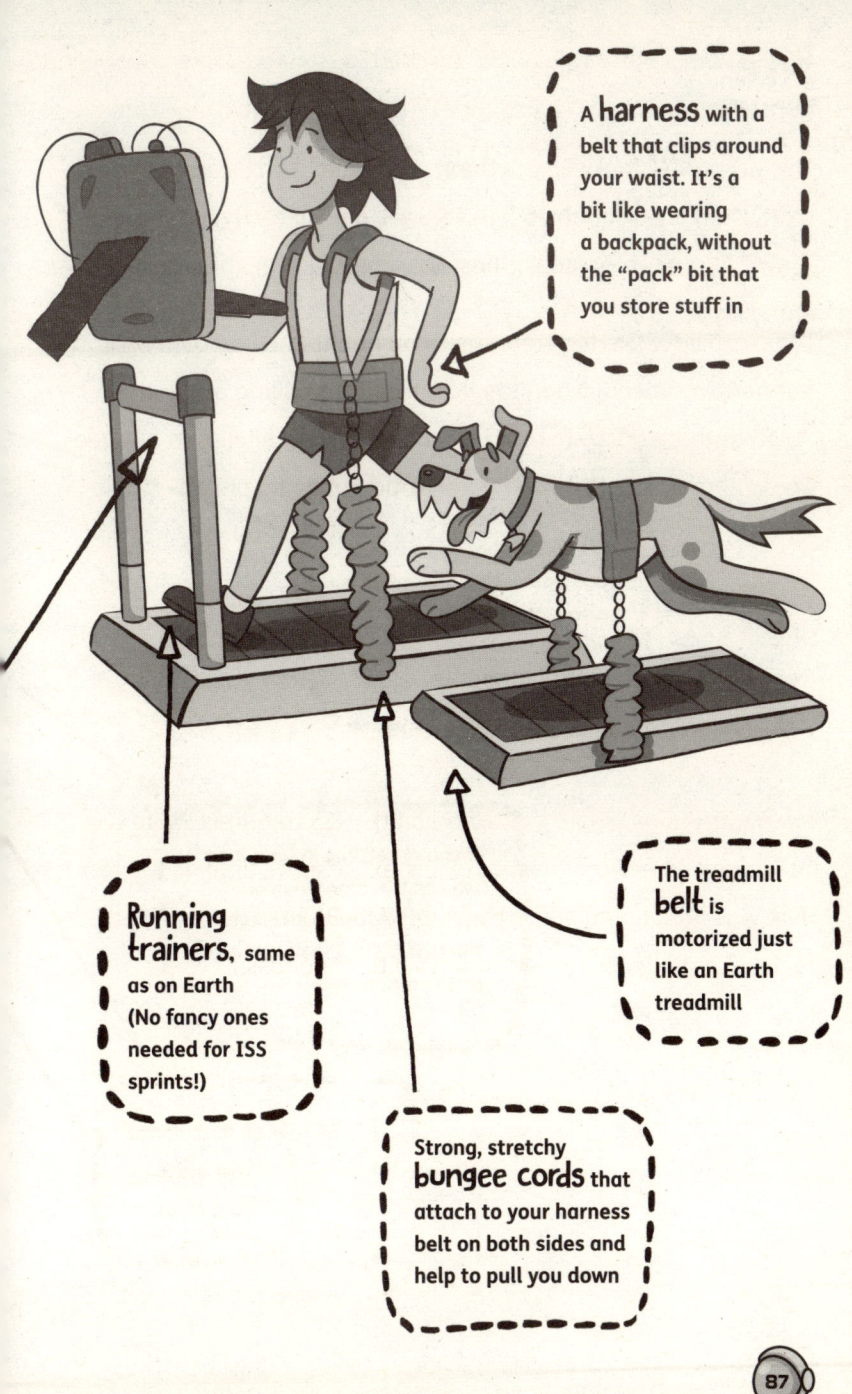

Bike

This does **NOT** look like anything you'd see in an Earth gym. For a start, there's no saddle, because, well, it's not really a thing to "sit down" in space! Instead, it basically looks like you're pedalling standing up. ☺

The anti-bounce frame attaches you to the ISS so that you don't end up floating around. It also stops bounce, because bounce is *not* good for a space station

If you're settling in for a long session (i.e. more than one episode of *Stranger Things*), the **back pad** makes things more comfortable

Handles to hold on to

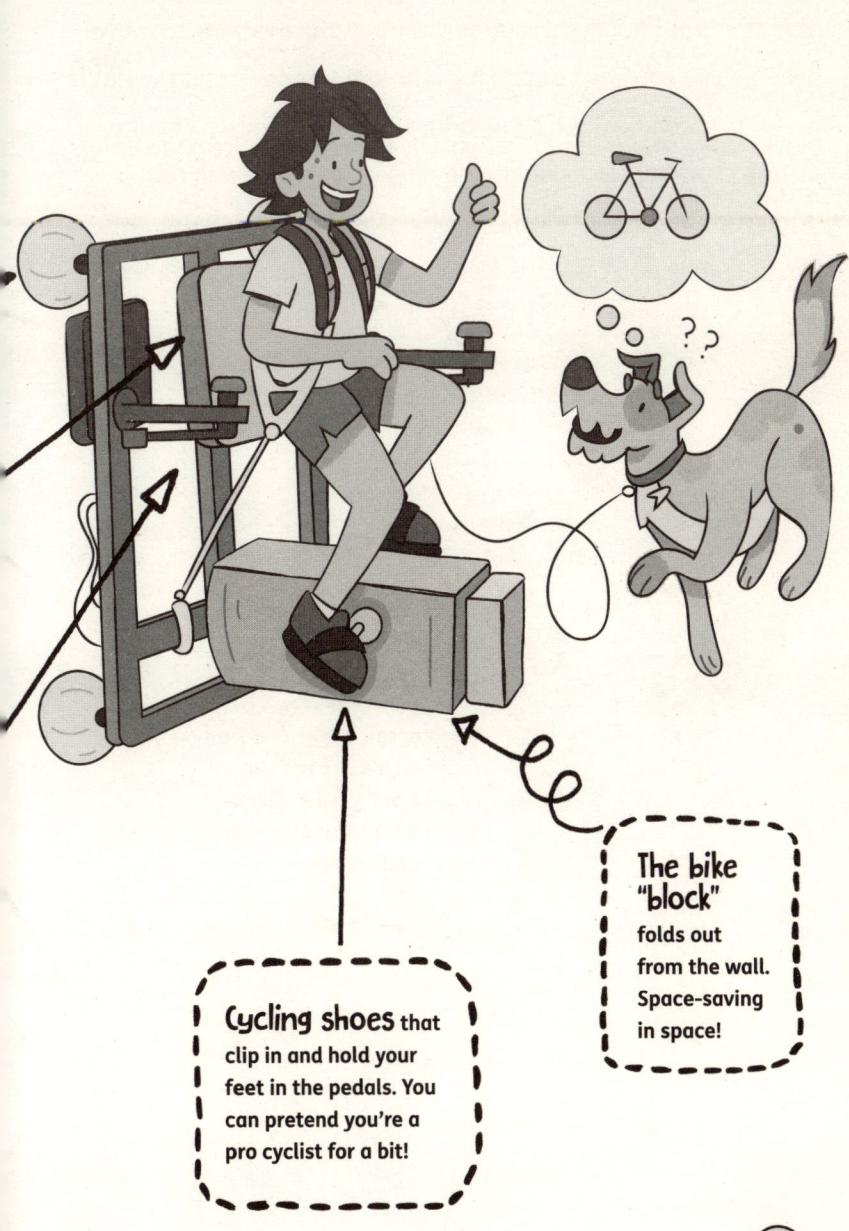

Cycling shoes that clip in and hold your feet in the pedals. You can pretend you're a pro cyclist for a bit!

The bike "block" folds out from the wall. Space-saving in space!

Another cool thing about our bike is that the whole set-up is part of a **Vibration Isolation System,** which means it's on a frame that bounces about and enables the machine to move with you as you work out. Same with the treadmill and the **ARED** weights machine (Perri's favourite – coming up next). The frame is taking on the forces created by the action of cycling rather than the structure of the ISS itself absorbing them. Because we definitely don't want the ISS bouncing around...

ARED (Advanced Resistive Exercise Device)

This is Perri's happy place. I'm pretty happy here too, as I know my bones and muscles are really benefitting from the resistance training we can do on this very cool piece of kit. It's got vacuum cylinders that provide resistance to pull against, making the **ARED** exercises feel like they would if you were lifting weights on Earth. (Remember the microgravity thing? The floating that's actually falling? That's why people and objects appear weightless – including actual weights you would want to lift...)

Using all the different attachments – like bars and pulleys and straps – we can do a whole range of exercises on the **ARED**. And best of all? Its location on the ISS means that when you're lying on your back doing a bench press you can look directly across to the Cupola and out to Earth. Talk about gains with a view!

Squats

Upright row

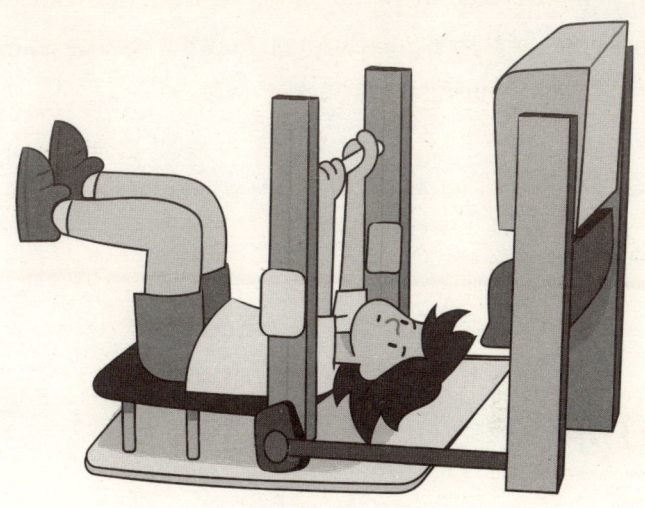

Bench presses

Shoulder presses

Right, I'm off to sweat* in the Tranquility module. (Ha! Could there BE a less appropriately named location for what we'll be doing in there? 😊) Send help if I'm not back in an hour!

*You know how I said astronauts drink their own – and everyone else's – pee (sort of)? Well, same goes for sweat... It also gets recycled into drinking water. Cool and gross, all at the same time!

8:30 pm

Phewwwwww. I survived Perri's Personal Training bootcamp, you'll be pleased to hear. (Actually, I loved it, but whatever happens, he must NEVER know that – his ego's already the size of Jupiter.) I started with intervals on the treadmill, which basically meant Perri yelling at me to go really fast, and then slow down for a bit, and then go really fast again, and then slow down for a bit. It's supposed to be a more efficient way of gaining fitness, although it felt like all I gained was a tomato face while the ISS gained about a gallon of drinking water.

While Perri trained on the ARED we had a lovely chat about how his astronaut training is going. Maybe my brother is a human being after all.

Oh, and then the best bit! Mum joined in and took us to Kibo (the JAXA module) where she taught us a yoga class. Mum does yoga on Earth to help her stay strong and keep her muscles loose for marathon running, but she says it's also great for staying calm and happy on the ISS. And it might even help us with getting used to being back in gravity when we go home, as you're improving your balance and coordination when you practise yoga. **Bonus!**

We went to Kibo because there's more room in there for big poses like Triangle, but it turned out that Perri needed more than room – someone's clearly been neglecting their stretching back on Earth... At one point during Crescent Moon pose he lost his foothold and floated away! I laughed so hard I almost peed.

I had **THE** best time at bootcamp today. And tomorrow, I get to do it all over again!

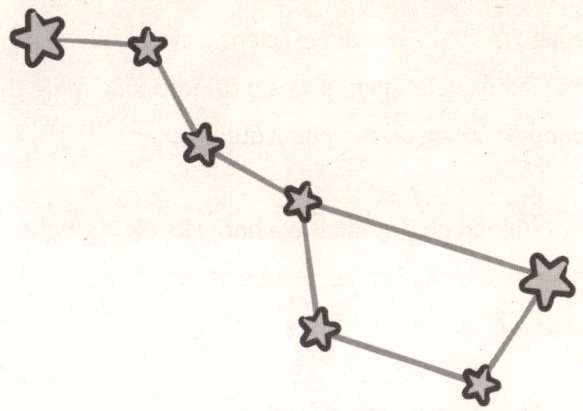

ASSIGNMENT
NUMBER SIX

Space Yoga

1. Planetary Pat-Down
Wake up and energise your body.

- Rapidly pat yourself all over for around a minute – down each arm; the inner part of your arms; your sides; chest; abdomen; the fronts, insides, outside, and backs of the legs; your bum; and your back.

- Gently pat your scalp.

- Then use your fingertips to patter all over your face.

> If you're practising on the ISS, don't forget to tuck your toes under a foothold!

2. Deep Space Breaths
Lengthen your spine, stretch the sides of your body, and make space for your lungs to expand and your diaphragm to move as you breathe deeply.

- Stand with your feet hip-distance apart and your arms down by your sides.

- Exhale.

- Inhale as you sweep both arms up sideways, reaching up at the top and keeping your shoulders down. Look up to your hands as you reach.

- Exhale and lower the arms back down.

- Repeat 3 times. Keep the movement in time with the breath.

3. Fold to Earth

Release your back and get a nice stretch through your hamstrings.

- From a standing position, slowly roll down your spine towards the Earth. Keep a slight bend in your knees.

- Let your arms and head feel heavy and feel your spine start to lengthen.

- You can also try gently swaying side to side at the bottom.

> Astronauts will need the help of their stretchy exercise bands to help them fold in microgravity!

- Slowly roll up to standing.

- Repeat 3 times.

4. Crescent Moon

Stretch the muscles between your ribs while you strengthen your core. It's also great for improving shoulder mobility.

- Stand with your feet together and sweep your arms up overhead, so your palms touch.

- Inhale and lift through your sides.

- Exhale, leaning over to one side and making a crescent moon shape with your body.

- Take a deep breath. Then come back to centre and try the other side.

5. Cosmic Camel

Stretch and open your chest, stretch your abdomen and hip flexors, and increase the mobility in your spine. It'll feel great!

- Stand with your feet hip-distance apart.

- Place your palms at your lower back for support, drawing your elbows together.

- Slightly bend your knees. Then curl your shoulders up and back as you lift your chest and steadily arch your back.

- Exhale as you gently release yourself into the arch a little more.

- After 2-3 breaths, slowly roll back up to standing.

- Stand still for a moment and take a nice deep breath as you absorb the benefits of the pose. 😊

6. Extra-Terrestrial Triangle

Strengthen your legs and back while opening up your shoulders and chest, AND enjoy a nice stretch for the muscles in your hips, thighs, and waist.

- Step one foot forward and one foot back, nice and wide. Make sure your back foot is at 90 degrees.

- Stretch your arms wide, and look out over your front outstretched arm.

- Move your body forwards as if someone is pulling you by your front hand.

- When you can't go any further, tilt down, taking your front hand to the inside of your ankle.

- Stretch and open the chest as you look up to your top hand. Take 2-3 breaths.

- Gently come back up to stand the same way you went in, and repeat the pose on the other side.

> Triangles on the ISS
> will need more of
> those stretchy
> exercise bands...

7. Out of This World Warrior

Strengthen your legs and open your legs, hips, and chest.

- Step one foot forward and one foot back, nice and wide. Make sure your back foot is at 90 degrees.

- Bend into your front leg, keeping your knee in line with your ankle and heel.

- Stretch your arms wide and look out over your front outstretched arm.

> Every Space Warrior needs her trusty exercise bands for this pose, too.

8. Supersonic Butterfly

Enjoy an inner thigh and groin stretch and hip-opener to finish.

- Sit up straight on the ground, with your spine nice and long.

- Bring the soles of your feet to touch and let your knees drop out to the sides.

- Gently flutter your knees up and down like butterfly wings to encourage more release in your muscles.

- Smile – you're a Space Yogi!

CHAPTER SEVEN

11:00 am

- - - - - -

I'm so excited, diary! It's Dad's 45th birthday today, and Mum, Perri, and I have been planning a really cool surprise for him for a while now. Mission Control Centre is involved and everything. (CLUE: It's not birthday cake with candles, because it's far too dangerous to have naked flames in space!*) I can't wait to see Dad's face when we surprise him at his birthday lunch later. Everyone on the station is invited, although Mum said some of the astronauts might be too busy with experiments and their other jobs to come. Taking time over your food and drink is less of a priority when there's science to be done... 🙂

*Although, cool fact – a flame is pretty much the shape of a sphere in space. Some Chinese astronauts once tried it under strict science experiment conditions.

The time astronauts have (or maybe I should say **don't** have!) for their meals is just one of the things that is taken into consideration when it comes to preparing our food for the International Space Station. The food scientists back on Earth have to think of lots of other things too:

Good nutrition – if astronauts have top nutrition to fuel their bodies, they'll be able to give their top performance in all the experiments and tasks they have to carry out.

Lightweight and compact – the food has to be transported from Earth, and the space and weight available in the cargo modules is really limited, so the lighter and smaller the better!

Great taste – I think this one's most important! 😊 (Wonder if the food scientists would agree?) Great tasting food makes an astronaut's life on board the ISS much more enjoyable.

Long-lasting – some of this food has to last as long as 18 months while staying nutritious and without going mouldy!

No crumbs – remember how you'd never want drops of water going astray on the ISS? Same goes for crumbs. Nothing good will happen if crumbs get into the computers! (We have yummy flour tortillas instead of bread, but I still miss crisp sandwiches **SOOOOOO** much.)

To help with all this, there are different ways that food is prepared for us back on Earth before it's sent to the ISS. One method is freeze-drying, which really helps with weight as it basically means sucking out all the water from the food. (Plus, no water means those tricksy bacteria that can make food go bad – and give us a nasty tummy ache – will find it tricky to grow.) We then add water back to the pouches of freeze-dried food in space to make it soft and squidgy again, and nice in the mouth. The other method is **thermostabilising,** where the food is heat processed (we're killing the bacteria off this time!) and then packaged in air-tight pouches. We can warm those up in an onboard food warmer or just eat straight from the pouch. 🙂 The method used depends on the type of food. One of the scientists told me that food that has a lot of dairy in it (mmm, cheese) tastes better in space if it's freeze-dried.

Okay, all this talk of food is making me hungry, and like all good hobbits, I need a second breakfast. **Back soon – with snacks**.

11:30 am
- - - - - -

Good news! My favourite snack of all was available this morning. It's a fruity, seedy, superfood-y energy bar packed with nutritious ingredients that Mum's friend – the amazing Chef Stefano – designed especially for us to take to space (the other astronauts on board worked with their own chefs). I even got to practise making some with Stefano in the food lab back on Earth before we left! Whenever I eat one of these snack bars, it makes me feel like I'm home. 🙂

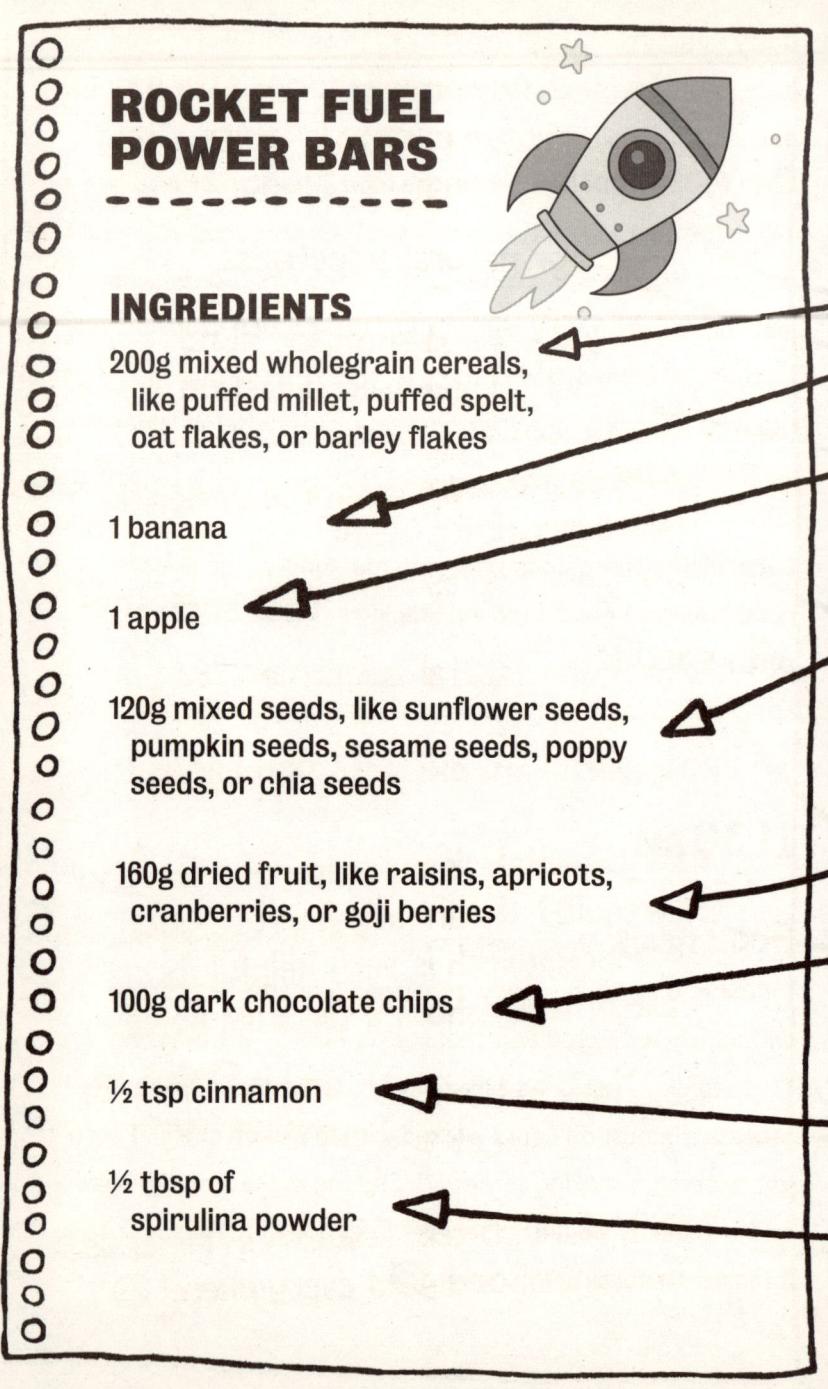

ROCKET FUEL POWER BARS

- - - - - - - - - - -

INGREDIENTS

200g mixed wholegrain cereals,
    like puffed millet, puffed spelt,
    oat flakes, or barley flakes

1 banana

1 apple

120g mixed seeds, like sunflower seeds,
    pumpkin seeds, sesame seeds, poppy
    seeds, or chia seeds

160g dried fruit, like raisins, apricots,
    cranberries, or goji berries

100g dark chocolate chips

½ tsp cinnamon

½ tbsp of
    spirulina powder

Wholegrains provide long-lasting, slow-release energy to stop you getting hungry again quickly

For natural sweetness

Keep the skin on for fibre, which helps with digestion

Seeds are a great source of healthy fats, providing energy and minerals that our bodies need to stay healthy

For more natural sweetness. Did you know, goji berries are one of the most powerful antioxidants you can eat?!

Dark chocolate is actually good for you (result!). It can help improve your mood, which is very helpful for astronauts who are far from home.

Another antioxidant, and it tastes sort of sweet and warming. Yum.

Very high in protein and rich in minerals. That superfood gets everywhere! ☺

Warning!

METHOD

1. Preheat the oven to 150°C.

2. Mix together the cereals, the seeds, cinnamon, and the spirulina powder in a large bowl.

3. Add the dried fruit and the chocolate chips and mix again.

4. Chop the banana and apple into small pieces and place in a saucepan with a small glassful of water (around 180 ml). Cook on a gentle heat for 15–20 minutes until the fruit is soft.

5. Add the softened banana and apple mix into the dry ingredients and mix thoroughly until everything is combined.

6. Line a 25 cm x 33 cm baking tin with greaseproof paper and evenly spread the mixture to a thickness of about 1–1.5 cm. Try to shape it into a square or a rectangle to make it easier to cut into slices.

You can fold in the sides of the parchment sheet to help you shape it!

7. Place another sheet of baking parchment on top and press down on the mixture to compress it and make sure it's even. Remove this sheet before baking.

8. Put in the oven and bake for 8 minutes.

9. Remove from the oven and cut into 16 slices while still soft.

Don't be tempted to eat any yet... It needs to firm up a bit first.

10. Leave to cool for 30 minutes. Then tuck into a slice and be powered up until your next meal!

YUM ☺

The Power Bars can be part of our special bonus food allowance, which every crew member gets. We can ask for our favourite snacks in our allowance, as well as meals that are just for us and made from our favourite ingredients. Stefano helped us design those too! The food scientists check that the food will be okay in space (nothing crumbly), and if it's a snack we would normally get from the shop they will buy it and then put it into special ISS-friendly packaging for us. Perri asked for pizza, but he forgot the no bread rule!

The rest of our food comes from a list of choices that we taste-tested at Mission Control Centre before we left for space.

(**THAT** was a very good day, I can tell you... 😊) We had more than 200 items we could choose from – even desserts. The list included food from the other countries working on the ISS too, so I've discovered some new dishes that we now eat up here as a crew. (Special shout out to Japan. I thank you from the bottom of my stomach for your outstanding milk candies.) And Mum was very keen to talk about what coffee she'd get in space.

Which reminds me... I promised to explain how the **Water Recovery System** works on the ISS, where pee gets turned back into drinking water. Yesterday's coffee becomes tomorrow's coffee. (Ha!)

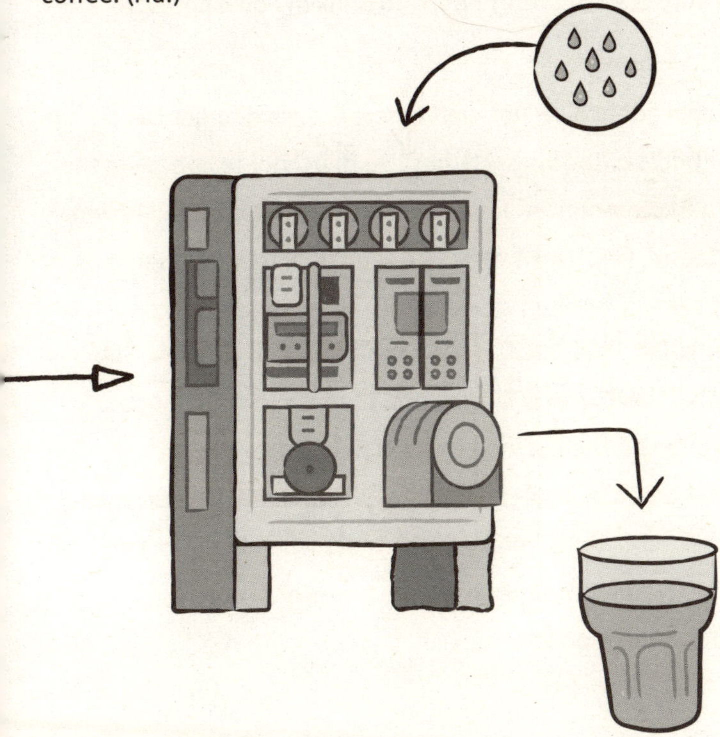

There are actually two parts to the system:

 The Urine Processor Assembly, where the water is extracted from the pee (pee is 95% water!) by distillation.

 That dirty water then joins the rest of the water collected by the air conditioning system on the ISS – like the water in our sweat and breath – in the Water Processor Assembly. It gets processed and treated until all the nasties are removed, and then it comes out the other end as clean drinking water or water for making coffee! It's actually purer than the water from the tap at home, so in space I'm totally happy to drink my own pee. ☺

Oh! I've only got half an hour left before we need to get things ready for Dad's birthday lunch, but I've **ALSO** got to complete my seventh assignment from Ms Asimov and send it back to Mission Control Centre. Eek. (Need to work on my time management.)

Assignment Number 7 is to create a menu for an astronaut... Wait! Why don't I make that astronaut me? I've been on the ISS long enough now to know what my favourite meals are, and – **bonus!** – it'll mean I'll never forget the space food choices I enjoyed the most when I get back to Earth. Then, when I'm sent on my next mission, I can just ask for the same menus!

ASSIGNMENT NUMBER SEVEN

A Menu for an
Astronaut-in-Training

Breakfast

Tvorog (Russian cottage cheese) with
blackcurrant purée squeezed from a tube

Mid-morning snack

Macadamia nuts (which always taste
better when thrown one by one and
caught in the mouth)

Lunch

Quinoa salad with dried tomatoes,
creamed leeks, and mackerel,
spread on a soft tortilla

Mid-afternoon snack

Dried apple slices

Dinner

Chilli shrimp cocktail
(my dulled tastebuds
appreciate the chilli kick)

Turmeric chicken,
mushrooms, rice,
and peas

Sweet red bean paste with chestnut
(thanks again, Japan!)

Okay, my assignment is done, so now I just need to find the ISS's bag of party hats and decorations and then it's off to Unity, where we always gather as a crew when we want to eat together. It's not really a kitchen, but there's a fold-down table that we can stick our food pouches to with hook-and-loop tape, a water dispenser for rehydrating freeze-dried goodies, and a food warmer to heat up the meals we don't want to eat cold. Oh, and I mustn't forget to bring my long-handled spoon! It's essential for scooping out every last bite from the pouches. ☺

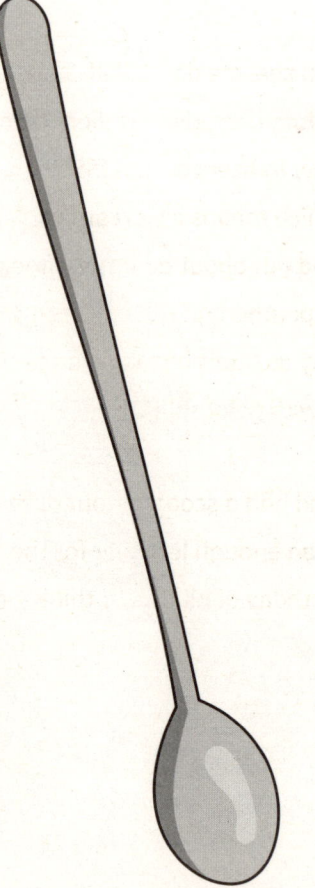

Wish me luck for Dad's surprise – I know he's going to **LOVE** *it*...

3:00 pm

Just call me Daughter of the Year. **No... Daughter of the Century!** Dad loved his surprise so much he cried. (And it's not all that nice to cry in microgravity, as tears sort of form a salty ball that just sit there on your eye until you wipe them away. Sorry, Dad!)

You see, my dad's half-Italian, and because of that, he says that *gelato* (incredible Italian ice-cream) runs in his veins. But the only freezers on the ISS are reserved for science experiments, which means ice cream can't be on the menu. Unless... you find out about an empty freezer being brought up for a new experiment in the next cargo module, arriving the very same day as Dad's birthday, and talk Mission Control Centre into filling it with gelato!!! ☺

Dad had a scoop of four different flavours, and there was still more than enough left over for the rest of us. He said it was his favourite birthday of all time. I think it might have been mine, too. ☺

CHAPTER EIGHT

7:00 am

I've just woken up to the sound of an alarm. That can't be good. I'm a little bit worried, but I'm going to do what it says on the T-shirt I'm sleeping in: **DON'T PANIC!**

7:03 am

There's a lot of hustle and bustle outside my crew quarters. At least, as much hustle and bustle as there can be when people are floating. The alarm's still going.

7:07 am

Douglas – unsurprisingly – is sleeping through the alarm, so I'm going out to see what's up.

7:50 am

Okay, so the alarm has now stopped, thankfully, but we're not in the clear yet. In between conversations with Mission Control Centre, Dad told me that one of the pumps on the cooling system on the outside of the International Space Station has failed, and without it, we risk overheating. A bunch of the equipment on board will be shut down to help keep things cool in the meantime, but it's going to require an **EVA** (AKA a spacewalk) to fix the pump.

A spacewalk! (I should NOT be excited right now – we're in the middle of an emergency situation – BUT, just between us, dear diary, could this be my moment? My big chance to complete my mission to go on an EVA before we return to Earth?)

10:10 am

It is not.

I tried **SO hard,** but there was no convincing Mum (or even Dad, who is normally a total soft touch) that I was ready to go on a spacewalk. They said it's because I've done hardly any EVA training.

To be fair, it is super intensive – astronauts do, like, years and years of preparation for an EVA back on Earth. (Yeah, I know. Probably should have thought of that when I was picking my mission.)

Of course, I reminded my parents I did do that one **epic** session in the Neutral Buoyancy Lab, which is basically a life-size re-creation of the ISS on the bottom of a **HUGE** swimming pool. From the surface of the water, it's like you're looking down on a small submerged city! **It's the coolest thing.** You get into a spacesuit and go more than 12 metres down to the bottom of the pool with scuba divers and practise different tasks and scenarios. Being underwater in the pretend ISS is the closest astronauts can get to practising in a bulky spacesuit before they go to space.

I mean, I was only allowed to explore a bit, and the suit was **SOOOO** hard to manoeuvre (forget about being able to bend your arms or turn your head sideways – you have to move your whole body if you want to look anywhere other than straight ahead), but I was still pretty good! **I stayed down there for two whole hours!** But then Mum reminded me that most training sessions last around six hours, are utterly exhausting to fully grown astronauts, and they have to do loads of them before they're qualified to do an EVA in space.

HMPH!

Not going to pretend I'm okay with this. It doesn't matter that what Mum and Dad say makes perfect sense. It means I'm going to fail to complete my mission, and I'm not going to get to qualify early to be an Astronaut-in-Training. I'm doomed to be a Space Flight Participant FOREVER! **WAHHHH.**

Although, I suppose all that's irrelevant if we boil to death in the ISS anyway. 😖

11:40 am

I know, I know – we're totally not going to boil to death, and I may have been a *tiny* bit dramatic in my last entry. We have the biggest brains from all the space agencies helping us out from Earth, all the astronauts on board have trained for every possible emergency situation, and my parents are awesome and are going on an EVA to fix the pump.

And even though I don't get to join them out there this time, Mum said I can be in their Spacewalk Support Team! Which means I get to help them suit up in the airlock. And that's the **next** coolest thing to going out myself.

Okay, time to remind myself how a spacesuit works so I can make triple sure I'm doing everything to keep Mum and Dad safe. Ms Asimov has just switched my next assignment to spacesuit revision, and now it's even more important I get **TOP marks!**

ASSIGNMENT
NUMBER EIGHT

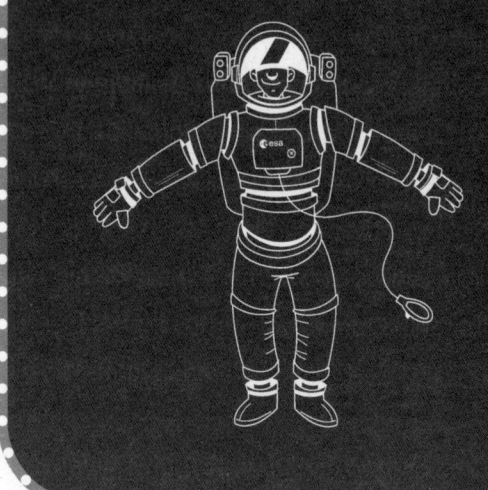

EMU (Extravehicular Mobility Unit*)

* the fancy name for a spacesuit!

Because an astronaut can be out on an EVA for many hours, the EMU has a lot of jobs to do:

- It stops them getting too hot or too cold (outside the ISS it can range between around 120°C when in the sun's light and around -160°C in the shade).

- It provides water and oxygen and takes away the carbon dioxide that the astronaut is breathing out.

- It's a communication system, so astronauts out spacewalking can talk to each other or to their crew on the ISS or Mission Control Centre.

It's basically a human-shaped mini spacecraft!

Cooling garment

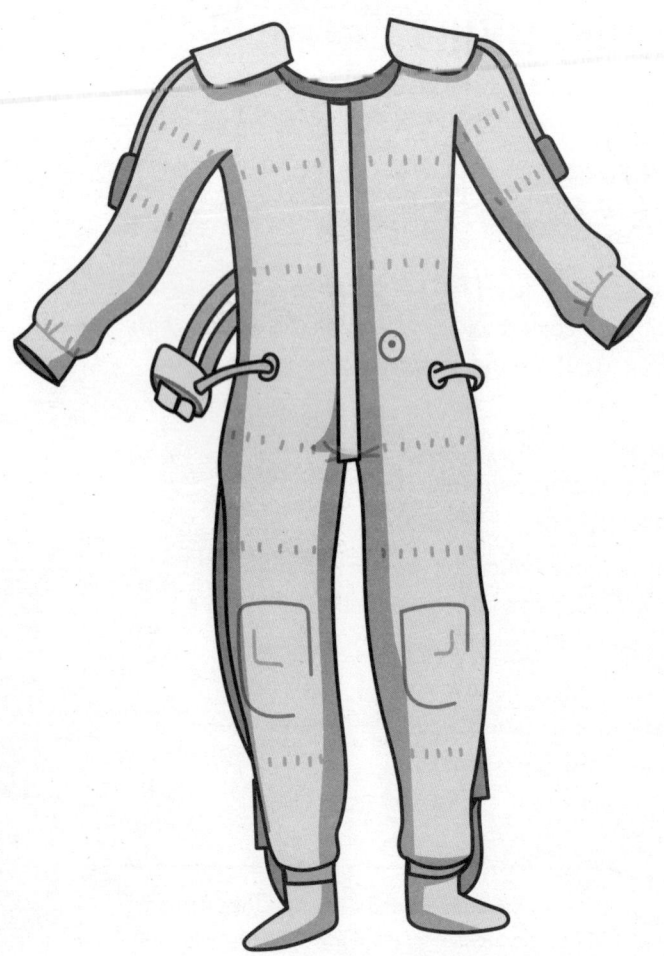

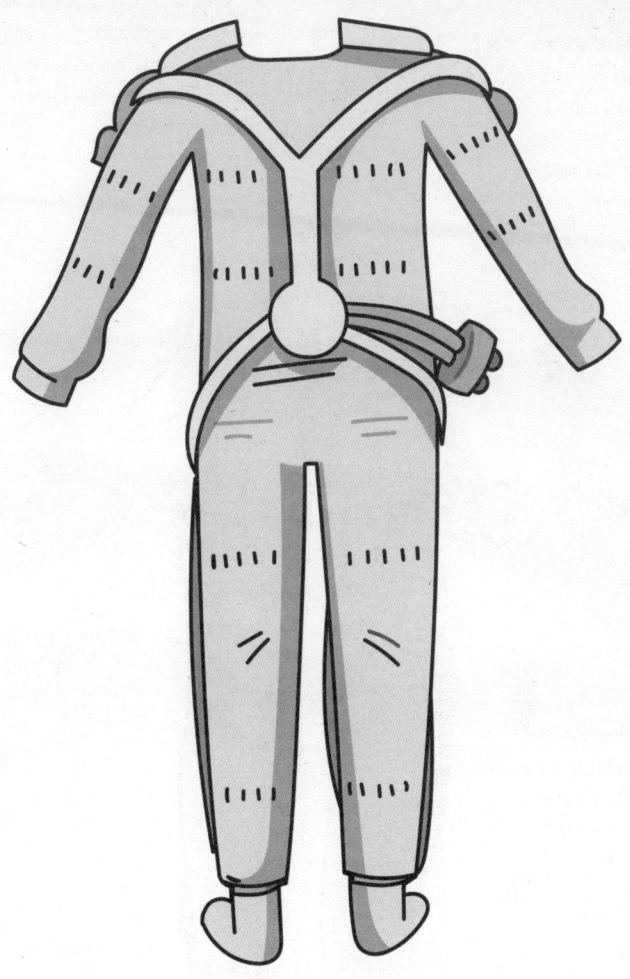

A high-tech onesie lined with more than 90 metres of flexible tubes. Cooling water flows through the tubes, and because it's close to the skin, it keeps the body's core temperature comfortable.

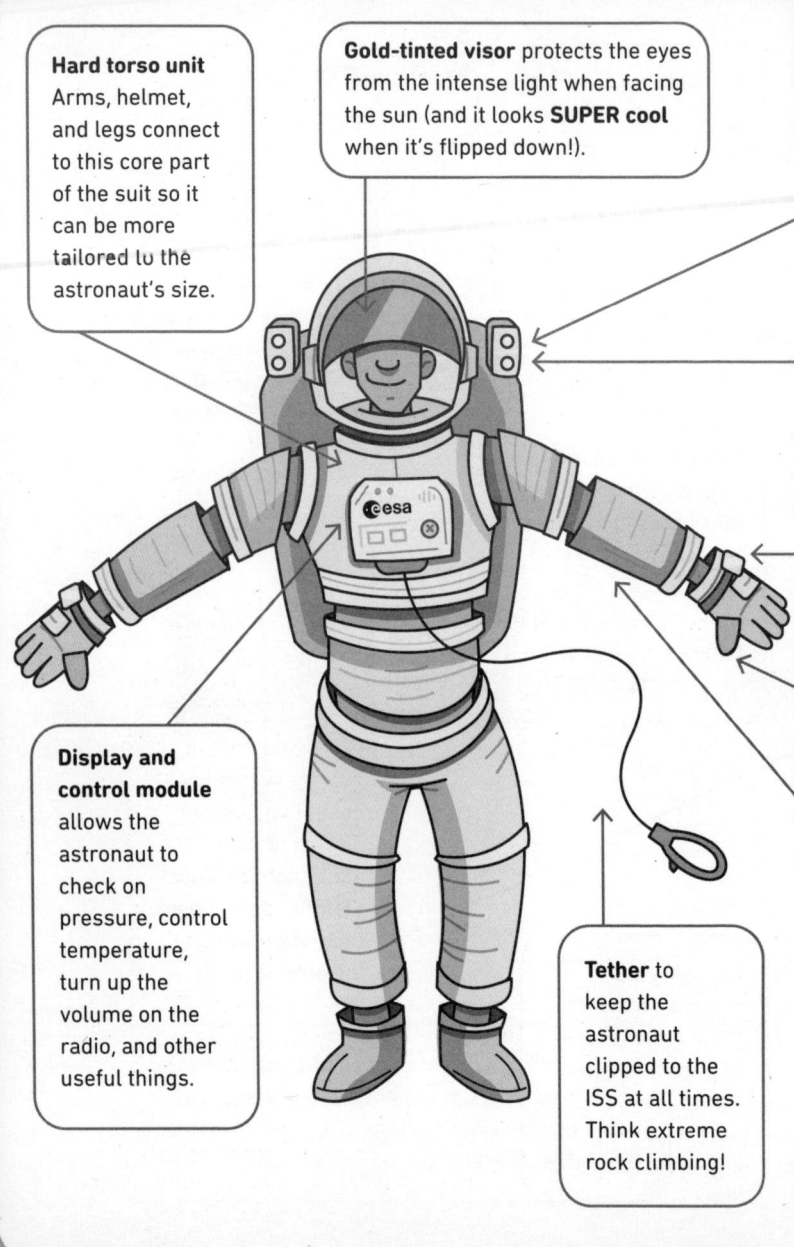

Hard torso unit Arms, helmet, and legs connect to this core part of the suit so it can be more tailored to the astronaut's size.

Gold-tinted visor protects the eyes from the intense light when facing the sun (and it looks **SUPER cool** when it's flipped down!).

Display and control module allows the astronaut to check on pressure, control temperature, turn up the volume on the radio, and other useful things.

Tether to keep the astronaut clipped to the ISS at all times. Think extreme rock climbing!

Cameras so everyone else can see what the astronaut is seeing and doing, from Earth as well as inside the ISS.

Spotlights Astronauts see the sun rise and set 16 times each day from the ISS, so they'll be working in the dark several times over on a long EVA!

Small wrist mirror to help read the numbers and words (all written backwards) on the display and control module. Astronauts can't bend over to check their dials in a spacesuit.

Gloves It's vital to keep hands mobile on an EVA, and not just for tasks – astronauts also use their hands to move themselves around the outside of the ISS. To help keep fingertips nimble, there's a heater inside the gloves.

Including the cooling garment, there are **14 layers** to a spacesuit (but astronauts don't have to put 14 individual suits on!).

Primary Life Support System (PLSS)

This is a backpack that literally keeps you alive, as it's where your fresh oxygen and cooling water come from and where the pressure in the suit is controlled.

There's also an emergency jet pack in case something goes **REALLY** wrong with the tether and you end up floating away from the ISS. There's about 20 seconds-worth of nitrogen gas in there to give you a one-shot chance of being propelled back to safety!

3:30 pm

EVAs take a while to prepare for, even the emergency kind. I've done my revision, and I'm ready to be the best Spacewalk Support Team member ever. Going to read some *Hitchhiker's Guide* while I wait.

4:50 pm

Still waiting.

6:00 pm

Stilllllll waiting.

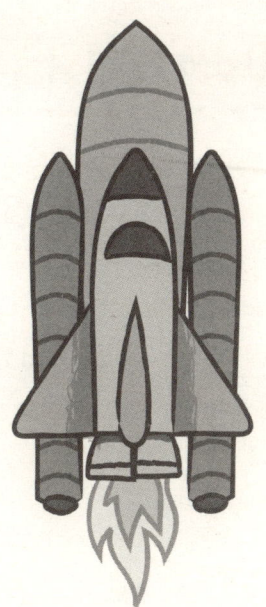

6:20 pm

Mission Control Centre has advised we're **"go"** for tomorrow morning. Apparently, even that's quicker than most other EVAs that have happened on the ISS. Dad says that right now there are people in the underwater version of the ISS back on Earth testing out the exact procedure for fixing the pump, so everything can be checked and ready for Mum and Dad's EVA by the time we wake up tomorrow morning.

Time for dinner and then an early night. **Got a very important job to do in the morning!**

9:00 pm (EVA day!)

There's so much to write about, I don't even know where or how to start, but... **it has been THE BEST day of my life!**

We started so early that I'm surprised I'm still awake. Mum, Dad, another crew member, and I entered the first part of the Quest Airlock, which is the module of the ISS with the hatch that opens straight out into space. This part of the Quest Airlock is called the Equipment Lock.

In there, I helped Mum and Dad get into their EMUs, connecting all the pieces of the suit together and checking everything was on properly. And checking again. And again. (They'd be dead verrrrry quickly if any part of them was exposed to space – like, unconscious within 12 seconds and dead in two minutes – so thorough checks are pretty important!)

Meanwhile, Mum and Dad were breathing pure oxygen and doing light exercises to help get rid of nitrogen in their blood and avoid the dangerous decompression sickness (caused by nitrogen bubbles forming in the body when pressure changes rapidly).

When everyone was happy with their suits, my parents floated into the second part of the Quest Airlock, the Crew Lock, and that's where we had to say goodbye. The hatch door to this lock was then sealed shut and the air removed, so it matched the lack of air outside the ISS. Mum and Dad tethered themselves and then the door to space was opened and they floated out of the Crew Lock to start their work.

Oh, I wish I could have gone out with them. **BUT,** the next best thing happened... a call came in from Ms Asimov to confirm that my vital contribution to the EVA as part of the Spacewalk Support Team would be considered a completed mission!

I'M GOING INTO EARLY ASTRONAUT TRAINING WHEN WE GET BACK TO EARTH!!!!

9:00 am

Does time pass quicker in space or something?* It's just that **SIX MONTHS** have gone by already, and it's now time for us Futuras to return to Earth. I really, really, really don't want to leave yet, but because I'm going into early astronaut training **(YESSSSS!)**, at least I know I'll be back in space someday... ☺

* It doesn't. I've just been having way too much fun!

Of course, I can't wait to give my nan the biggest hug, and take Douglas for a proper walk (on the ground!), and see my best friends. Kelsi, Dorian, Ava, and Audrey don't know it yet, but I brought some friendship bracelets with me so they can all have a gift that has been to actual space!

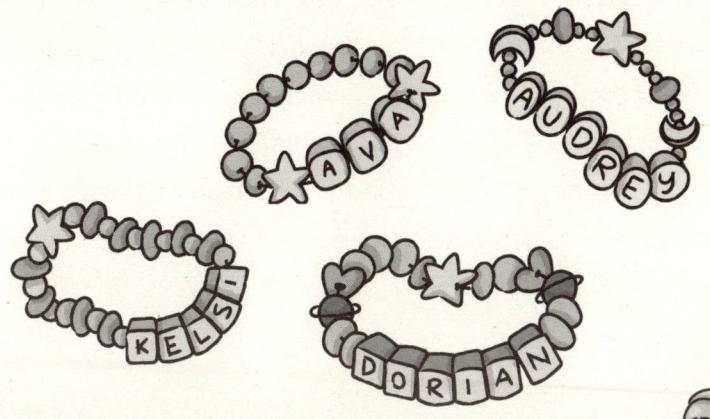

This morning's going to be a bit boring though. It's time for clean-up. Dad gave me and Perri a lecture yesterday about not leaving a trace of ourselves on the International Space Station so that the next astronauts to arrive have a clean and tidy new home. While Mum and Dad are busy reviewing their re-entry manuals, I'm going to be vacuuming our crew quarters. **I don't even want to think about how many of my brother's toenail clippings I'm gonna find. BARF.**

I've promised myself a trip to the Cupola later though, as a reward for all the cleaning. I'm going to take my piece of stromatolite with me for one final visit to the place where I get to have the whole of Earth as my backyard.

3:30 pm

Phew, I've been busy. I finished cleaning every nook and cranny of our quarters (not many toenails, which either means they're merrily floating around the ISS or Perri did listen when I was telling him about suction). Then I did a slow cartwheel in the Service Module a) because I could, and b) I wanted to make sure the feeling of moving my body so effortlessly is imprinted on my memory. I mean, cartwheels are always fun, but this has to be the **funnest** one I'll ever do.

137

And then - you're never going to believe this - I went to the Cupola, and just as I was about to leave, **I saw the Northern Lights!**

I mean, I've watched the sun rise **SO** many times from this viewing window in the last six months. The first time, I told Mum it reminded me of an egg yolk sitting there on the horizon, and she said she wished I hadn't said that because it was now going to make her dream of fried eggs for the entire mission. (Eggs only come freeze-dried on the ISS, and they're a bit... grim.)

I've seen the way the ocean changes from one shade of blue to the next, like colouring pencils lined up in order in their tin. I've even been able to pick out the boot shape of Italy, where my Grandpa Futura's from. But literally nothing has made my jaw hit the floor quicker than looking out on the dancing, shimmering, swirling multi-coloured light doing its thing in front of us. Even Dougie couldn't look away.

It felt like space was putting on a goodbye fireworks display - or maybe it was Earth welcoming us home. Whichever it was, I don't think I'll ever see anything more beautiful in my life.

5:00 pm

Nearly time to leave. I've put on my **MAG** (Maximum Absorbency Garment and Perri's favourite bit of kit: the nappy. Don't worry – we get a fresh one for the return journey!) and have hugged all the crew that are staying behind on the ISS. There's still a final job or two for the rest of my family to do, but all I have to worry about now is putting on my custom-made suit and taking my seat inside the vehicle that will speed us back to Earth.

Perri and Dad are carefully packing the Crew Dragon for our departure. They have to follow very particular instructions from Mission Control Centre for where everything is placed, from our personal stuff to the science experiments that are hitching a ride with us to Earth-side laboratories. It's because the centre of mass in the vehicle has to be **JUST RIGHT** for us to be able to re-enter the Earth's atmosphere at the right angle. We definitely don't want to be popping back out the other side into space again (if the angle's too shallow) or burning to a crisp (if it's too steep).

Mum's sort of watching but also trying not to interfere, like she does when Dad's packing the car for a camping trip. **Ooh! Camping!** Maybe we can go when we've all recovered from re-entry. I've forgotten what the smell of grass and the feel of fresh air is like.

Anyway, anything that's not packed in those bags can't be sneaked in before we leave. Which means, dearest diary, it's time for me to say goodbye and I'll see you soon. **Next time I write in you, we'll have fallen back on to our planet!** But before I stash you safely in my kit bag, I just want to make sure I write down what Ms Asimov said to me earlier today in our final video chat. I never, ever want to forget these words – and I know they're gonna come in handy in the future, 'cos I've got big, Mars-shaped dreams...

"If you have an ambition, take motivation from that, and apply yourself to the utmost. Choose the most difficult path, the one that allows you to grow. It's important to have a dream for the journey, not for the finish line."

So this is Astronaut-in-Training Andromeda Futura, signing off.

For now...

Dear Nan,

It's me, Andi! I know we're going to see you soon, but I wanted to write to you anyway as we're not doing much here at Mission Control Centre other than having tests done and trying to get used to gravity again...
AND I know how much you love getting a proper letter from me in an envelope through your letterbox!

I'm going to post this to you tomorrow. Actually, I'm going to ask Ms Asimov if she'd mind posting it for me, because when I try to walk, my legs still feel like two twigs trying to hold up a boulder. 😊

Recovering from being in space is hard, Nan, but it's **100 million per cent** worth every second I spent on the ISS – even though my brain is struggling to keep up with how my body needs to move on Earth and my bum cheeks feel sore when I sit down. (I haven't sat down on anything for six months!) I also accidentally broke our doctor's phone. I borrowed it just for a second, but when I went to give it back I forgot that it wouldn't float and sort of let it go, expecting to be able to give it a gentle push in her direction. **Oops**.

I didn't really like the journey back though, and I'm glad Mum had given Dougie some medicine to help him sleep through it too, because he **DEFINITELY** wouldn't have liked it. (You know how he hides in the saucepan cupboard when there's thunder.) When the trunk of the spacecraft detached – because it had done its job and wasn't needed anymore, so it detached from the crew module to get burned up in the atmosphere – there was a jolt that felt like I was being punched hard in the back. The best way I can describe the noise is like we were surrounded by snarling monsters trying to get in and eat us. And I got the same sensation of being forced back into my seat as on the journey out to space, but it felt **WAY** worse on the flight back because my body was used to weightlessness. It was **SO** hard to breathe – although I did do the special breathing exercises Mission Control Centre had taught me in Spaceflight Participation training, and that helped a bit.

BUT you'll never guess what...! Perri figured out I was scared and was amazing about it. (My brother's **totally** been possessed by an alien who's kind to little sisters.) He even got me to close my eyes for the bit towards the end when we were surrounded by flames, thanks to the spacecraft speeding through the air and causing enormous heat. He realised it would freak me out, even though we were **totally protected by a heat shield!** (Although the heat scorched and blackened the windows so much that I couldn't have seen out of them even if I'd wanted to.)

I guess what I'm saying, Nan, is that even though I might have to pay for a new phone screen out of my pocket money and I'll need to get used to angry monsters, and punches in the back, and being on fire, and heavy people sitting on my chest, I will go back to space one day. I've **GOT** to go back!

Oh, I nearly forgot. Is there room in the pond at your allotment for something new? It's an epic algae called spirulina, and I know a lot about it now... we could try to grow it together. 😊

Parachutes to help us slow
down and hit the water gently

**Us splashing down in the ocean before
the rescue team came to get us.**

Can't wait to see you soon!

Love, Andi xxxxxx

GLOSSARY

Andromeda constellation = A constellation of stars that was named by the Ancient Greeks after a mythological princess.

Closeout crew = The closeout crew are the last non-crew members astronauts see until they return to Earth. The closeout crew are responsible for strapping astronauts in and closing and sealing the crew access hatch.

Commander = The commander of the International Space Station inhabits the ISS. They are responsible for telling the other crew members what activities to do, updating the Flight Director at Mission Control Centre, and keeping the crew and the ISS safe.

Deep Space = So far, the furthest astronauts have travelled is to the side of the moon that we can see from Earth. The areas of space beyond our moon are called Deep Space.

Distillation = A technique for separating the liquid from a mixture so that the liquid part can be kept.

Launch Director = The Launch Director plans and oversees the countdown and lift-off of a spacecraft. They make the final decision if a launch goes ahead or not.

Microgravity = The condition in which objects or people appear to be weightless. The effect of this is that objects and astronauts float. "Micro" means "very small", so there is still some gravitational pull in space.

Mission Control Centre = The direct link between Earth and the ISS. The team here provide support 24 hours a day, 7 days a week. They communicate with and monitor ESA astronauts aboard the ISS to make sure that they are safe.

Orbit = A regular, repeating path that one object takes around another object, e.g. the path that the Earth takes around the sun. Satellites are the objects in an orbit. Satellites can be natural, e.g. the moon, or human-made, e.g. the ISS.

Robotic probe = Robotic probes are launched from Earth into space to explore and gather information. They are unpiloted and uncrewed. Some probes make one-way journeys and use radios to communicate what they find. Others return to Earth with their data and samples.

The International Space Station (ISS) =
A space station is a spacecraft that remains in orbit. The ISS is the largest space station ever built, and is operated by the space agencies of Europe, the US, Japan, Russia, and Canada. There has been human presence on the ISS for more than 20 years.

WHAT IS
THE ESA?

esa

→ THE EUROPEAN SPACE AGENCY

About the European Space Agency

Simply, the European Space Agency's (ESA's) role is to put together and carry out the European space programme. The ESA's space programme aims to:

 Find out more about Earth

 Discover more about our solar system and the universe

 Develop and advance satellite-based technologies and services

ESA's headquarters are in Paris, France, but the organisation has specialist facilities across Europe, including the European Astronauts Centre in Germany, the European Space Research and Technology Centre in the Netherlands, and the European Centre for Space Applications and Telecommunications in the UK.

Twenty-two countries are Member States of ESA. They are:

Austria, Belgium, Czech Republic, Denmark, Estonia, Finland, France, Germany, Greece, Hungary, Ireland, Italy, Luxembourg, the Netherlands, Norway, Poland, Portugal, Romania, Spain, Sweden, Switzerland, and the United Kingdom.

Slovakia, Slovenia, Latvia, and Lithuania are Associate Members; Bulgaria, Croatia, Cyprus, and Malta have cooperation agreements with ESA; and Canada participates in some projects under a cooperation agreement.

Around 2,200 people from across the Member States work for ESA, including scientists, administrators, IT specialists, and engineers.

ESA is funded by contributions from all Member States, and in 2023 had a budget of just over €7 billion.

MEET
SAMANTHA

Samantha Cristoforetti was born in Milan, Italy and studied in Italy, Germany, France, and Russia.

In 2001, she joined the Italian Air Force Academy, graduating in 2005. From there she joined the Euro-NATO Joint Jet Pilot Training program in the US and earned her fighter pilot wings in 2006.

Samantha was chosen as an ESA astronaut in 2009 and completed her basic astronaut training in November 2010. She first travelled to the International Space Station in 2012 as part of the crew of Expedition 42/43.

Samantha returned to the ISS as part of the Minerva mission in April 2022 where she was responsible for the American, European, Japanese, and Canadian modules and components. During this expedition, Samantha was the first European woman to undertake a spacewalk and the first European female to command the ISS.

When she's not travelling for work, Samantha lives with her partner and two children near ESA's Astronaut Centre in Cologne, Germany. She enjoys learning foreign languages, and when she has the time she loves to hike, practise yoga, scuba dive, and re-read her favourite book: *The Hitchhikers Guide to the Galaxy.*

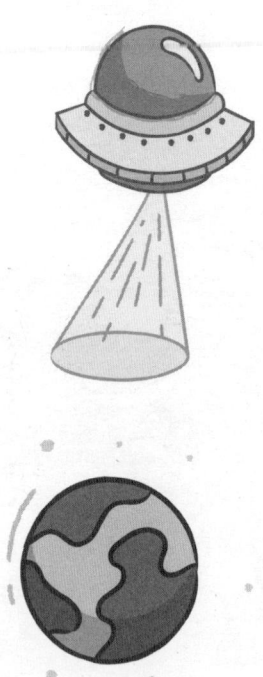

Project Editor Vicky Armstrong
Project Art Editor Chris Gould
Senior Production Editor Jennifer Murray
Senior Production Controller Louise Minihane
Senior Acquisitions Editor Katy Flint
Managing Art Editor Vicky Short
Licensing Managing Director Mark Searle

Designed for DK by Anita Mangan
By Samantha Crisoferetti with Emma Roberts
Illustrations © Doug Fuchs, 2024

DK would like to thank Julia March for proofreading;
Charlie Donaldson and Alisha Comber at Rocket Licensing;
and Nadia Lueders and the rest of the team at the ESA.

The European Space Agency is not a manufacturer or distributor of the
product. ESA authorised the branding of the product
with the ESA name, acronym, and/or logotype.
Licensed by Rocket Licensing on behalf of the ESA.

First published in Great Britain in 2024 by
Dorling Kindersley Limited
DK, 20 Vauxhall Bridge Road, London, SW1V 2SA

The authorised representative in the EEA is
Dorling Kindersley Verlag GmbH. Arnulfstr. 124,
80636 Munich, Germany

A CIP catalogue record for this book is available from the British Library.
ISBN: 978-0-2416-8381-1

Printed and bound in the United Kingdom

www.dk.com

**DK would like to thank the following for their
kind permission to reproduce their images:**

Back Cover: ESA - P. Sebirot; **i:** NASA; **ii-iii:** ESA/NASA/Roscosmos; **iv:** ESA/
NASA-S.Cristoforetti/ R. Rossi; **v:** ESA/NASA; **vi-vii:** ESA/NASA; **viii:** ESA/NASA